THE ALL AMERICANS

THE ALL AMERICANS

The 82nd Airborne

Leroy Thompson

A David & Charles Military Book

DEDICATION

This book is dedicated to York who, though he never jumped out of a perfectly good airplane, always displayed courage and loyalty in the best airborne tradition.

Jacket photographs
Front: Members of the 82nd Airborne Division parachute from a C–130 Hercules aircraft during the joint exercise Bright Star of 1983.
Back: Aboard a C–141 Starlifter aircraft, members of the 82nd Airborne hook up in preparation for an air-drop over Germany during Reforger 1982.
Official US Air Force photographs

British Library Cataloguing-in-Publication Data

Thompson, Leroy
The All Americans; the history of the
82nd Airborne Division.
1. United States. Army. Airborne Division
82nd to 1988
I. Title
358.4'00973

ISBN 0-7153-9182-8

© Leroy Thompson 1988

Typeset by Typesetters (Birmingham) Limited
and printed in Great Britain by
Butler & Tanner, Frome
for David & Charles Publishers plc
Brunel House   Newton Abbot   Devon

Distributed in the United States by Sterling Publishing
Co. Inc., 2 Park Avenue, New York, NY 10016

CONTENTS

ACKNOWLEDGEMENTS

The author would like to thank the following individuals and organizations for assistance in preparing this book: Air Force Office of Public Affairs, Lou DiPonziano, Hal Feldman, Pete Geery, Pete McDermott, T.J. Mullin, Courtney Phelps, Harry Pugh, XVIIIth Airborne Corps, 82nd Airborne Division Public Affairs, and all the 'All Americans' throughout the years.

INTRODUCTION

I have wanted to write this book for many years because the lack of a comprehensive history of this, the United States' most famous fighting division, has been a significant omission. The 82nd Airborne Division offers a fascinating subject for the historian because its story spans much of the twentieth century from its inception as an infantry division in World War One to its current place as the key rapid deployment unit in America's strategic reserve. By no means, however, can the 82nd be viewed only as an historical entity; its position in American military planning is too critical for that. The history of the 82nd Airborne Division continues to grow, the most recent combat chapter being written during the invasion of the island of Grenada.

The 82nd has had its share of famous officers and men, from Sergeant York to 'Slim Jim' Gavin, but this is really the story of the unnamed guys in jump boots, baggy pants, and – most recently – maroon berets who have always been willing to jump into danger and then drive on until the objective was secured. The two most common nicknames for the 82nd – America's Honorguard and All Americans – in themselves say something about the important place the only current American airborne division holds in the hearts and minds of Americans, their friends, and their enemies.

Leroy Thompson

1 'LEGS', BUT TOUGH ONES

So famous has the 82nd become as an airborne division that its proud World War One heritage as a conventional infantry division is sometimes forgotten. When the United States declared war on Germany on 6 April 1917, the 82nd Division was not even in existence, but by the end of the conflict less than two years later, the 82nd would have seen more continuous combat than any other US division and would have suffered almost seventy-five per cent casualties.

Formed on 25 August 1917 as part of the massive growth of the US Army towards a goal of one million troops in France by May 1918, the 82nd Division was raised at Camp Gordon, Georgia, under Maj Gen Eben Swift. Since members of the division came from all forty-eight states of the Union, the unit was given the nickname 'All American', hence its famed 'AA' shoulder sleeve insignia. Members of the division, in fact, were even more diverse than their regional origins might indicate since at one point almost twenty per cent of the inductees assigned were of foreign birth. However, many of these were later weeded out as 'enemy aliens.'

As it formed, the division was divided into two infantry brigades and one artillery brigade: the 163rd Infantry Brigade composed of the 325th and 326th Infantry Regiments and the 320th Machine Gun Battalion; the 164th Infantry Brigade composed of the 327th and 328th Infantry Regiments and the 321st Machine Gun Battalion; and the 157th Artillery Brigade, consisting of the 319th, 320th and 321st Field Artillery Regiments and the 307th Trench Mortar Battery, plus various attached units including the 307th Engineers.

Although the rapid growth of the US Army caused grave equipment shortages which forced the 82nd Division initially to train with wooden rifles, the All Americans did receive intensive training in the methods of trench warfare from French and British officers as well as American officers. Shortage of machine guns and grenades also forced the doughboys of the 82nd to spend extra time training with their bayonets, always a good method to build aggressiveness.

'Up the line to death. . .'

Training completed, the first members of the division sailed for Europe on 25 April 1918. On the way to France, they passed through England, where the 325th Infantry Regiment was reviewed by His Majesty the King in London. After arriving in France, the 82nd Division went into training immediately with the weapons they would use in combat, a training to which the nearness of battle gave a sense of urgency. By June, a few officers and NCOs were receiving 'on the job' combat training in the front

Sergeant Alvin York, highly decorated hero of the World War I 82nd Division (*National Archives*)

lines with their British allies. As a result of this combat orientation, the 82nd suffered its first combat death when Capt Jewitt Williams of the 326th Infantry Regiment was killed on 9 June.

Other members of the division would soon join Williams as battalions from each regiment moved into the front line trenches in the Lagny Sector on 25 June 1918. The first battalions in the line were the 2/325th, 1/326th, 3/327th and 2/328th; other battalions remained in support or reserve. Artillery support was provided by the French because the 82nd's own artillery units were still receiving additional training behind the lines in France.

However, the division's own machine gun battalions moved into the line in mid-July. Before long, the hours of intensive bayonet drill and raid training were also put to the test as members of the 82nd Division carried out their first night raid on 4 August. By the time the members of the 82nd Division were pulled out of the Lagny Sector on 10 August, the All Americans were already well blooded and had suffered 374 casualties.

After moving into position the 82nd Division relieved the 2nd Division in the Marbache Sector on 15 August. Joined then by the 157th Artillery Brigade in this sector, the 82nd now had their own divisional artillery support rather than having to rely on the French for heavy firepower. This sector had developed a reputation for being somewhat quiet – both sides had, in fact, used it to rest units who had seen heavy combat – but the 82nd found that for them, at least, it was not all that calm. In addition to frequent artillery and air bombardment, the troopers found themselves having to deal with aggressive German patroling.

It was just as well, however, that the Germans kept the All Americans sharp because the division was selected to take part in the first major US offensive of the war at St Mihiel. Operating on the right flank of the southern portion of the advance, the 82nd was assigned the village of Norroy as an objective. They occupied it, meeting virtually no resistance. Although this objective was easily taken, the division suffered a total of 950 casualties during the offensive, which lasted until 21 September 1918. One of the seventy-eight killed was the divisional machine gun officer, Lieutenant Colonel (LTC) Emory Pike, who won a posthumous Congressional Medal for Honor for rallying disorganized men of the 328th Infantry and then going to the aid of a wounded man under fire.

The Meuse-Argonne Offensive

On 24 September, the division relocated again, this time to the Clermont area west of Verdun, the scene of the most bloody battle in history, which had raged throughout 1916 and cost almost one million lives. Acting as the reserve for the US 1st Army, the 82nd was not initially committed to the Meuse-Argonne Offensive, which began on 26 September. The respite did not last long, however, as the first divisional element – the 327th Infantry Regiment – was committed to shore up the defenses near Apremont on 29 September. After only one and a half hour's notice, the men of the 327th made a forced march to move into the line and then held their ground against stiff German pressure for two days until relieved by the 1st Division.

On 4 October, the remainder of the division joined the 327th Infantry near Varennes. On this same date, Maj Gen George B. Duncan took command of the All Americans, relieving Brig Gen William P. Burnham. Two days later, the 82nd moved back into front line positions, replacing the 28th Division. Back on the offensive on 7 October, the division's 164th Brigade launched an attack against the Germans, seizing Hills 180 and 223 against tenacious resistance. One small incident during the 164th Brigade's drive would make one man of the 82nd Division the most famous American soldier of the war.

Sergeant Alvin York

During this push by the 164th Brigade, on 8 October, one battalion – the 2/328th Infantry – was assigned to infiltrate through the German lines near the town of Chatel-Chehery on Hill 223. During this advance, the battalion was halted by heavy machine gun fire, resulting in G Company receiving orders to silence the enemy machine guns. As has happened throughout the history of warfare, a small detachment of infantrymen were at the sharp end, drawing the actual assignment of silencing the German automatic weapons. Consisting of four NCOs and thirteen privates, this patrol began a stealthy advance on the German positions with a crafty Tennessee woodsman named Alvin York at the point. So skilfully did York guide the patrol that they surprised about seventy-five Germans, who, not realizing how greatly they outnumbered the Americans, soon surrendered, though Corporal York, the point man, had to kill one of the Germans who resisted.

Other German machine gunners, however, were less intimidated by the few Americans and opened up with their Maxims, killing nine of the patrol, including three of the NCOs. Only Corporal York and seven privates remained alive. While the privates took cover or concentrated on covering the prisoners, York made good use of the marksmanship skills he had acquired turkey hunting for the pot back in the hills of Tennessee. Carefully aiming his 1917 Enfield rifle, he killed numerous Germans. Realizing that York's rifle had only a five-round magazine capacity, a German lieutenant led five other men in a charge against York's position. The Germans, however, had not counted on York's shooting skill. York shot the last man first and worked forward until his Enfield ran dry and then drew his Colt Government Model .45 pistol to shoot the final man. York had demonstrated yet again that while a pistol may not be a particularly effective weapon of war, there are times in close combat when it is the difference between life and death, a fact appreciated by combat troops but rarely realized by rear echelon officers.

Finally, after York had killed twenty-five Germans, resistance ceased and the Germans surrendered. As York and his remaining six comrades marched their prisoners back, they added more to their take, eventually reaching their battalion with 132 Germans in tow. For his amazing feat of marksmanship and gallantry, York received the Congressional Medal of Honor, the Distinguished Service Cross, the French *Croix de Guerre* with palms and *Légion d'Honnuer*, the Italian *Croce de Guerra* and the Montenegran War Medal.

The great irony of York's accomplishment was that he had initially been a conscientious objector who had agreed to combat service only after intensive soul searching. Years later during the Vietnam War, York's heroism allowed the members of the 101st Airborne Division, friendly rivals of the proud 82nd Airborne, to kid their fellow paratroopers about the fact that the most famous soldier in their division's history had been a 'leg' infantryman, but even the 'Screaming Eagles' of the 101st had to admit he had been a hell of a soldier nevertheless.

Other regiments of the 82nd Division attacked north on 10 October, driving the Germans from the eastern half of the Argonne Forest. For the next three weeks, the 82nd held the ground they had gained until relieved by the fresh 77th and 80th Divisions, which moved in to replace the 82nd and continue the drive. During the Meuse-Argonne offensive the All Americans had performed impressively, but the butcher's bill had been high as the division suffered over six thousand casualties, including 902 killed.

Less than two weeks after the 82nd Division was pulled back, the Armistice went into effect on 11 November 1918. For the next three months, the division was assigned near Pravthay, France, where they carried out training and waited for orders home. Finally, on 2 March 1919, the All Americans began moving to Bordeaux; then, in April, the orders to sail for home finally came through. After arriving in New York, units of the division were demobilized. The division's deactivation was completed on 27 May 1919. During the war, the men of the 82nd had spent 105 days in the front lines during which time they suffered 1,035 killed in action; another 378 would die from wounds incurred in battle. In addition to the division's two Congressional Medals of Honor, three All Americans won the Distinguished Service Medal and seventy-five won the Distinguished Service Cross.

Twenty-Three Year Deactivation

For more than two decades, the 82nd Division would live on only in the memories of the men who had served in its ranks during World War One, but after the pernicious Japanese attack on Pearl Harbor on 7 December 1941, the 82nd Infantry Division was formed once again as part of the War Department's plan to expand the US Army to a strength of one hundred infantry divisions. Reactivated on 25 March 1942 at Camp Claiborne, Louisiana, under Brig Gen (later Maj Gen) Omar Bradley, the 82nd was initially trained as a standard infantry division under a training cadre drawn from the 9th Infantry Division. Both Maj Gen Bradley and his second in command, Brig Gen Matthew Ridgway, who became divisional commander on 26 June 1942, were exceptional commanders, and soon managed to imbue the division with a sense of purpose.

As a result, as training progressed, the 82nd proved itself one of the best in the entire army. To foster pride in the division, Bradley and later Ridgway stressed the division's proud World War One heritage, and on 7 May 1942 invited Sgt York to address the men. Realizing the esprit de corps of the 82nd and the capabilities of the division, the War Department at one point considered training the division as a motorized division. Instead, the 82nd was chosen to be another type of pioneer. On 15 August 1942, the 82nd Infantry Division became the first of a new type of division – airborne! Designated the 82nd Airborne Division, with half of its strength drawn off to form the second airborne division – the 101st Airborne – the new 82nd Airborne was ready to create a legend that has continued to grow for almost half a century.

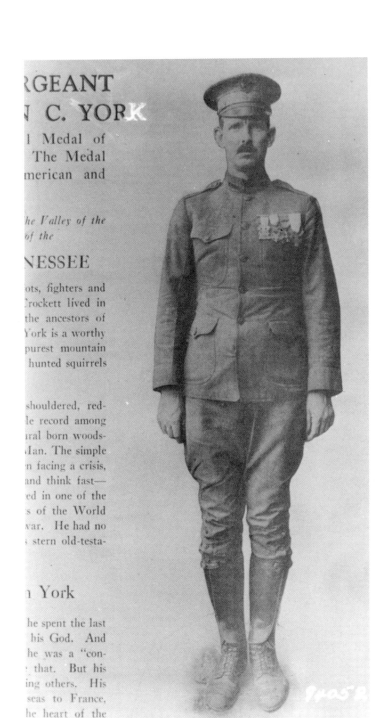

The heroic Sergeant Alvin York of the 82nd Division became the symbol of the doughboy for millions of Americans and an example for the men of the later 82nd Airborne Division. (*National Archives*)

2 AMERICA'S FIRST PARATROOPERS

Germination

The United States might have been the first country in the world to have airborne forces had air power visionary Billy Mitchell been heeded late in World War One. As early as 1918, Mitchell had suggested that the US 1st Infantry Division – fresh from the Meuse-Argonne offensive – be pulled from the trenches and trained as parachute troops so that they might be dropped, twelve-thousand-strong, behind German lines to spearhead an assault on the fortress of Metz. Foreseeing the need for firepower, Mitchell planned to organize his airborne division into 1,200 ten-man squads, each assigned with two .30 machine guns. For air transport, Mitchell foresaw the use of sixty squadrons of Handley-Page 0/400 and V1500 heavy bombers. Mitchell assigned a staff officer to prepare the detail plan for the airborne operation against Metz, LTC Lewis Brereton, who, in 1944, would command the 1st Allied Airborne Army during Operation MARKET GARDEN.

Mitchell, in fact, foreshadowed many of the German *Blitzkrieg* tactics in planning his assault on Metz. Once the parachute troops had been dropped behind the German defenses, Mitchell planned that they would be resupplied and given fire support from the air while they struck the Germans from the rear, as the enemy were attempting to deal with an attack on their front by tanks launched at the same time. Realizing the problem of scattering, which would plague future airborne forces, Mitchell worked on the assumption that as few as ten per cent of the assault force – 1,200 men – would actually make it into position for the assault.

However, before the plans had progressed very far, the Armistice was signed on 11 November 1918. Unfortunately, though Mitchell continued to write about the usefulness of airborne troops until his death in 1936, little post-war thought was given to the creation of US parachute infantry until the Soviets and Italians in Europe demonstrated their own parachute forces during the 1930s.

US officers who had seen demonstrations of the Soviet, and later the Italian and German parachute infantry capability, finally revived US military interest in the parachute as a method of inserting infantry during the late 1930s. With the expansion of the US armed forces during the late 1930s, Army Chief of Staff Gen George Marshall took note of the European interest in parachute troops and ordered Chief of Infantry Maj Gen George Lynch to make a study of the feasibility of forming a detachment of 'air infantry.' Initially, it was felt that such a unit would be trained to parachute in and seize an airfield for air-landing follow-up troops. This idea was obviously based upon observation of large-scale Soviet exercises involving such a scenario.

During their training members of the Parachute Test Platoon jumped from parachute towers in New Jersey, thus establishing this method of training for future paratroopers. (*US Army*)

Studies in the military frequently move slowly. However, the urgency generated by the approaching war in Europe resulted in the air infantry study being completed in less than a week. Lynch's study indicated that air infantry could be used for the following missions: small unit raids in enemy territory (Lynch felt it necessary to point out that these might include suicide missions); reconnaissance missions in enemy territory; raids to seize and hold a bridgehead or other key installation ahead of advancing forces; and scouting missions ahead of advancing mechanized forces. Lynch further recommended that experiments be carried out to determine organizations and equipment for such a unit.

After reviewing the recommendation, Marshall passed it on to Maj Gen 'Hap' Arnold, the Chief of the Air Corps, for evaluation in light of transport capabilities. Late in September 1939, just a few weeks after the invasion of Poland, Arnold received a recommendation from the Commandant of the Air Corps Tactical School that an air infantry unit should be formed, but within the Air Corps. In terms of function, this unit, it was argued, would bear the same relationship to the Air Corps as the Marine Corps did to the Navy. Two possible names – 'Air Grenadiers' or 'Air Corps Grenadiers' – were optimistically suggested for the unit. Other subordinates, however, argued that the Air Corps lacked sufficient transport aircraft to support air infantry, no matter which branch they fell under. Consequently, Arnold recommended to Marshall that the air infantry idea be temporarily shelved, a measure which Marshall approved.

The idea did not remain dormant for long. The Soviet use of parachute troops against Finland late in 1939 brought the air infantry concept to the fore once again, receiving high priority by January 1940. With the Chief of Staff now behind the idea, Maj Gen Lynch assigned forty-three year old Major Bill Lee, one of his staff officers, to head the new project. With the air infantry project now moving rapidly, in February 1940, the Infantry Board submitted a recommendation that work begin on developing a troop parachute and, once it was developed, that an infantry platoon drawn from volunteers be formed to carry out test jumps.

The Air Corps carried out development work on the parachute at Wright Field, Ohio, resulting in the T-4 static line chute, while at Fort Benning, Georgia, other tests were carried out. Although the air infantry project was already moving through its preliminary stages quite well, the program really shifted into high gear after the Germans demonstrated just how effective airborne troops could be as parachute and glider troops spearheaded the *Blitzkrieg* into the Low Countries in May 1940. As a result, on 25 June 1940, the order was received at Fort Benning to provide volunteers from the 29th Infantry Regiment – the demonstration unit for the Infantry School – to form a test parachute infantry platoon.

The Parachute Test Platoon

As volunteers were sought for the initial parachute test unit over two hundred men applied for the thirty-nine enlisted slots, while seventeen lieutenants vied for the single officer's slot. Parachuting was considered so dangerous that only unmarried men were allowed to volunteer. Also allowing for the likelihood of injury, forty-eight unmarried enlisted men were eventually selected. Lt William T. Ryder, who had been an adherent of parachute troops for some time and who had written several studies on the subject, was selected to command the platoon.

Once selected, the members of the Test Platoon were detached and given special assignment to the Infantry Board. The first course began in early July 1940. It covered parachuting, physical training and small unit tactics, and lasted eight weeks. Later American paratroopers who remember the grueling three weeks of their jump school with grimaces will certainly sympathize with the Parachute Test Platoon.

As would the tens of thousands of American paratroopers who followed them into harness, the Parachute Test Platoon spent hours learning PLFs (parachute landing falls) during the initial phase of training. One technique used to give more realism was having the trainees perform their PLFs from moving trucks, a method David Stirling later employed in the Western Desert when training the initial contingent of Special Air

During April, 1941, early Army parachutists check their harnesses. Note the jump suit and soft helmet worn at this stage. (*US Army*)

Service (SAS) parachutists. The rigid discipline and ten pushups for mistakes which would become staples of US parachute training started with the Parachute Test Platoon and continues right up to the present.

While the Parachute Test Platoon was learning the basics which would allow them to jump safely into battle beneath their new T-4 parachutes, Maj Lee oversaw their progress from Washington, making frequent trips to Fort Benning to monitor their training. One of Lee's greatest contributions was the discovery that the Safe Parachute Company in New Jersey had two 150ft (46m) parachute towers. Realizing the potential of these towers as training aids, Lee arranged for the Test Platoon to spend ten days at Fort Dix so that they could train on the towers. During tower training, Gen Lynch visited the fledgling parachute troops and even carried out a tower jump with them.

Once their tower training had been completed, the Test Platoon returned to Fort Benning to complete their training. By the end of the seventh week of training, the men were in outstanding physical condition, knew how to pack their own parachutes, jump, land and go into combat upon landing. However, they had yet to 'exit from a plane in flight' – the final stamp of approval for a paratrooper. Eighth week was to be jump week during which the Test Platoon would make five jumps. The Test Platoon had already established many traditions which would become part of the American Airborne mystique, but had still another to foster as the tradition of yelling 'Geronimo!' while exiting the aircraft originated with the Test Platoon during their jump week.

It was intended that the final jump of the unit's training would be used as a demonstration of the platoon's capabilities as they would stage a mock assault upon landing while VIPs observed. Such interest had this initial contingent of American parachute troops aroused, in fact, that the list of VIPs was much more impressive than anyone had expected, attracting Henry Stimson, the Secretary of War, and Gen Marshall, the Chief of Staff, as well as Gen Lynch, Chief of Infantry, and other high-ranking officers. Fortunately for the future of America's airborne forces the demonstration went well, the VIPs being suitably impressed by the descent from the sky and rapid assault of the ferociously howling parachute troops.

Training completed and their place in American Airborne history assured, the Parachute Test Platoon now provided cadre for the parachute

During training members of the Parachute Test Platoon quickly distribute weapons which they obtained from the weapons roll in which they were dropped. Note that each paratrooper jumped wearing a pistol. This method was probably copied from the Germans who did not jump with their primary weapons. By the time US paratroopers made their first combat jump, however, they were jumping with their weapons. (*US Army*)

training school at Fort Benning and the nucleus for the parachute-borne hordes which would help retake Europe and the islands of the Pacific. Only a few weeks after the Test Platoon completed their own training, in fact, they began training the first full parachute infantry battalion – the 501st Parachute Infantry.

Even before the Test Platoon had completed their training, infighting had begun between the Air Corps, which argued they should control parachute troops because they needed aircraft to deliver them to battle, the engineers, which argued they should control parachute troops since they would be trained in demolitions, and the infantry, which argued they should control parachute troops since they would fight as infantry once on the ground. Gen Marshall decided, however, that the parachute forces would remain part of the infantry. As a result, the first of the new parachute infantry battalions – the 501st – began training its complement of select volunteers under the command of Major William Miley.

Development of US airborne forces now continued at a frenetic pace as, in November 1940, the War Department decided to form three more parachute battalions to follow the 501st. Meanwhile, as the 501st Parachute Infantry Battalion progressed through training, US paratroopers received authorization to wear their first uniform distinctions as they were allowed to blouse their trousers into boots and to wear the overseas cap with circular parachute insignia. A 501st lieutenant, William Yarborough, also designed the US parachute brevet, which would be worn by all Army paratroopers in the future. Among Yarborough's other contributions were the design of the special parachutists' uniform with large cargo pockets and the design of special jump boots. Yarborough's interest in distinctive uniform items did not wane later in his career either, for as a brigadier general he played a key role in helping the Special Forces receive authorization to wear the green beret in the early 1960s and helped to design the jungle fatigues used in Vietnam.

July 1941 saw the activation of the second parachute battalion – the 502nd Parachute Infantry – and also the commencement of experimentation with the use of gliders to transport troops. Actually, 'Hap' Arnold had ordered the Air Corps Experimental Test Center to design a glider capable of transporting 12–15 troops on 4 March 1941. By July, four civilian companies were working on prototypes. Under Major Frederick Dent, the Glider Branch of the Aircraft Laboratory was established, and Dent and eleven other powered aircraft pilots received an initial thirty-hour glider flying course. To get the fledgling glider program started, 150 qualified power pilots were selected to receive glider training with the intention that they would act as the cadre to train future military glider pilots.

In August 1941, the 503rd Parachute Infantry Battalion was activated, followed by other battalions during the next few months. With the massive increase in manpower requirements for the new parachute forces, a Parachute School was activated at Fort Benning to carry out jump training.

It is interesting to note from the 1942 edition of *Essentials Of Infantry Training*, the Bible of the Infantry School, that the largest parachute organization discussed is the battalion. According to *Essentials*:

> In addition to the foot, motorized, tank, and antitank infantry soldier, there is still another type – the parachute infantry soldier.
> Parachute troops are organized into parachute battalions. The parachute battalion is composed of a headquarters, a headquarters company, three parachute companies, and attached medical personnel. Its strength is 36 officers and 482 enlisted men.
> **Headquarters and headquarters company.** There are six officers and three enlisted men in the parachute battalion headquarters. The headquarters company has a headquarters platoon, made up of a company headquarters section, staff section, and a mess section; a communications platoon; and a supply platoon composed of a parachute section, a battalion supply section, and a transport section. The strength of the headquarters company is four officers and 107 enlisted men. The headquarters company provides all the mess, supply, and records personnel for the entire battalion.
> **Parachute Company.** Each of the three parachute companies consists of a company headquarters and three rifle platoons. The company has eight officers and 119 enlisted men. Each rifle platoon is made up of a platoon headquarters, two rifle squads, and a 60mm mortar squad. The rifle platoon has a strength of two officers and 35 enlisted men. The platoon headquarters consists of a first lieutenant and a second lieutenant; a staff sergeant, platoon sergeant, a corporal, signal, radio, and code corporal; three privates first class or privates, one of whom is a radio operator and the other two messengers. The 60mm squad consists of a sergeant, squad leader, and five privates, first class, one of whom is the gunner, one the assistant gunner, and three of whom are ammunition carriers. The rifle squad is led by a sergeant. The corporal is the assistant squad leader, seven privates first class or privates are riflemen, one is a light machine gunner, one an assistant light machine gunner, and one an ammunition carrier.

The 7 December 1941 attack on Pearl Harbor galvanized the War Department. The authorized parachute infantry strength was increased even further as the War Department ordered that four parachute regiments should be formed in January 1942. The parachute regiments at this time had an authorized strength of 1,958 men and each was composed of three parachute battalions. For the later history of the 82nd Airborne Division, the fourth of the new regiments – the 505th Parachute Infantry Regiment was of special importance as it was commanded by LTC James M. Gavin, who would become a legendary commander of the division before the end of the war.

Pearl Harbor acted as a similar stimulus for the glider program, resulting in an increase on 20 December 1941 of the requirement for glider pilots to

Members of the Parachute Test Platoon having their chutes inspected prior to a jump. Note that the inspecting captain wears the parachute oval on his sidecap. (*US Army*)

1,000. This number stemmed from the belief at this point that seventy-five per cent of an airborne division would be glider-borne in 1,000 gliders while the other twenty-five per cent of the division could ride in the tow planes. However, since power pilots were also needed in abundance, it was decided that enlisted personnel with prior flying experience would be selected for glider pilot training. Even this expedient did not prove sufficient to meet manpower needs: on 1 April 1942, the requirement for glider pilots was raised to 4,200 and then a few weeks later to 6,000. To meet these manpower needs, the Civil Aeronautics Administration (CAA) was asked to help recruit pilots from among civilian pilots – both powered and glider. Even with the help of the CAA and the response of patriotic civilian pilots willing to enlist, the qualifications demanded of recruits were eventually lowered so that those with no prior flying experience were accepted for training. The number of glider pilots needed and the urgency of the demand also precluded carrying out the training at military facilities, which were already overburdened with the demands of training power pilots. Therefore, glider pilot training was carried out at civilian schools. While suitable gliders were coming into production, civilian-owned sailplanes were purchased and certain light powered planes were altered to non-powered configuration. Finally, in June 1942, the Waco CG-4A was accepted for production. The Waco, which had a hinged nose allowing a jeep or light artillery piece to be easily loaded or unloaded, became an important part of the new airborne divisions.

Realizing that the growing airborne forces needed a controling organization, Lt Gen Leslie McNair, the commander of American ground forces, ordered the formation of Airborne Command under Col William Lee in March 1942. Lee, realizing that the airborne forces under his command would continue to outgrow the facilities available to them at Fort Benning, moved Airborne Command to Fort Bragg the next month. Fort Bragg has remained the home of US airborne forces for the last four a half decades until the present.

The increasing number of airborne troops would, of course, need transport aircraft to deliver them to battle, so Troop Carrier Command was organized within the Air Corps at the same time as Airborne Command. The experimentation with gliders having proven their viability, in May 1942, the first glider infantry regiment – the 88th Glider Infantry – was formed. Equipped with Waco gliders and having a strength of 1,605 men based on two battalions, the 88th was the forerunner of future Glider Infantry Regiments which would join with the Parachute Infantry Regiments as the basis for airborne divisions.

A battalion of the 503rd Parachute Infantry achieved the distinction of being the first Army parachute unit to go to war when they sailed on 6 June 1942.

Realizing that the new airborne infantry would need artillery support, Airborne Command began experimentation in the summer of 1942 with a Parachute Test Battery which tested the methods of dropping demountable airportable artillery pieces. These could be broken down for parachuting and then reassembled rapidly on the ground by the paratroopers. Initially, the 75mm Pack Howitzer, designed for transport on mules, was selected for the parachute artillery units. The Test Battery's experiments having proven the viability of parachute artillery, the unit formed the basis for the 456th Parachute Field Artillery Battalion, the first airborne artillery unit, which was activated in September 1942.

To some extent in response to the British plan to form airborne divisions, the War Department made the decision in the summer of 1942 to activate two airborne divisions – the 82nd and the 101st. The 82nd Airborne Division was initially commanded by Maj Gen Matthew B. Ridgway. Among the initial units assigned to the 82nd were the 325th Glider Infantry Regiment, the 326th Glider Infantry Regiment, the 504th Parachute Infantry Regiment, the 319th Glider Field Artillery Battalion, the 320th Glider Infantry Battalion, the 376th Parachute Field Artillery Battalion, the 80th Airborne AA Battalion and the 307th Airborne Engineer Battalion. Under this organization, the division was intended to contain two glider infantry regiments and one parachute infantry regiment, but this was altered to one glider infantry regiment and two parachute infantry regiments due to the shortage of gliders. In consequence, in February 1943, the 505th Parachute Infantry replaced the 326th Glider Infantry Regiment.

As the elements of the new 82nd Airborne Division trained to forge themselves into the parachute-borne rapier from the sky which would eventually pierce the Third Reich, events in North Africa were taking place which would bring the All Americans into the war.

3 OFF TO WAR

Members of the 82nd Airborne undergoing physical training in North Africa in June 1943. (*US Army*)

Once the 82nd Division had been converted to an airborne division, intensive training was carried out, first at Camp Claiborne and then after 1 October 1942 at Fort Bragg. During the eight months between the conversion of the 82nd to airborne and the receipt of overseas orders, the 'All Americans' were brought up to full strength and intensively trained in the special tactics dictated by their new role as air delivered assault troops.

With all airborne insignia and their beloved jump boots removed to conceal their identity, the 82nd left Fort Bragg on 20 April 1943 for Camp Edwards, MA, in transit to the port of New York where they boarded transports on 27 April. Leaving New York on 29 April, the troopers of the 82nd Airborne Division set sail for North Africa, arriving twelve days later on 10 May in Casablanca harbor. From the harbor, members of the division were marched to Camp Don B. Passage. They stayed there for only a few days before being transported northeast to Oujda, where the paratroopers were to be bivouacked, and to Marnia, where the glider troops were to be bivouacked. The time spent in Morocco proved an excellent toughening period for the already rugged airborne troops prior to their entry into combat. Living under field conditions and carrying out practice jumps or glider operations, the troopers honed the edge that would soon draw its first blood against the Axis.

Although the 509th Parachute Infantry Battalion had already seen action during Operation TORCH, the 82nd was the first US airborne division to arrive overseas and the All Americans proved an attraction for visiting allied brass, with more than fifteen generals reviewing the division at Oujda, including Mark Clark (a long-time friend of the parachute troops), 'Tohey' Spaatz, George Patton, Omar Bradley and Dwight Eisenhower. As might be expected, an affinity was established between 'Blood and Guts' Patton and the tough paratroopers. Despite the visiting brass, however, the 82nd managed to cram a lot of training into the six weeks it spent at Oujda. Partially because of the extreme heat during the day time, many exercises were carried out at night, including compass marches and practice at reforming after parachute drops in the dark. Since combat drops were normally made at night, these exercises would prove invaluable later when the division went into combat. The 509th

An airborne engineer of the 82nd Airborne checks his mine detector in North Africa during June 1943. (*US Army*)

Parachute Infantry Battalion, veterans of three combat jumps in North Africa, were attached to the 82nd at Oujda, albeit reluctantly, since they felt their combat jumps made them superior to the newly arrived All Americans.

Although there was not much opportunity for entertainment at Oujda, the 505th Parachute Infantry did get a chance to acquire a replacement mascot for Max, the dog which had jumped with them in the States but was left behind when the unit deployed to North Africa. The new mascot was a jackass, which they unsuccessfully tried to teach to jump as well. Unfortunately, it broke a leg on the first jump and had to be shot.

On 16 June, the division began deploying to Kairouan, Tunisia, where the troopers were treated to further tough desert training in pursuit of the paratroopers' twin Holy Grails – leanness and meanness. For part of the division at least the baptism of fire was near. On 24 May 1943, Ridgway called Col Gavin to his HQ to inform him that his 505th Parachute Infantry would parachute into combat over Sicily on 9 July 1943. Gavin's troopers would act as the key element in a combat team from the 82nd which would spearhead the invasion of Sicily, Operation HUSKY.

At this time, a parachute regiment consisted of 2,029 men organized

At Oujda, members of the 82nd load equipment packed for parachuting into the bay of an aircraft prior to a training drop. (*US Army*)

into an HQ Company, a Service Company and three Parachute Infantry Battalions. These battalions had a strength of thirty-five officers and 495 other ranks. The battalion contained an HQ Company (seven officers, 138 other ranks, eight .30 LMGs and four 81mm mortars) and three rifle companies (each of eight officers and 119 other ranks). Each company was further broken into three platoons and each platoon into three squads plus a 60mm mortar squad equipped with one mortar. Armament for each battalion consisted of 505 .45 caliber pistols so that each paratrooper would have a weapon easily brought into immediate action upon landing, 101 M1 carbines, 325 M1 rifles, fifteen M1903 rifles for sniping, forty-five .45 Thompson SMGs, forty-four .30 LMGs, nine 60mm mortars and four 81mm mortars.

The lack of transport aircraft prevented both the dropping of all the 82nd's parachute troops and the use of glider troops on Sicily. However, the 505th would be augmented by a battalion of the 504th Parachute Infantry, the 456th Parachute Field Artillery Battalion and Company B of the 307th Airborne Engineers. The remainder of the 504th would parachute in on D+1 to reinforce the 505th. According to the plan, 266 C-47s would carry the regimental combat team to their drop zones near Niscemi, ten miles north-east of Gela on the southern coast of Sicily. The paratroopers' mission would be to secure the roads leading to the beaches where the American amphibious assault would strike and to secure their drop zones for follow-up drops. Though lightly armed, the paratroopers would be expected to hold their objectives until they had linked up with the US 1st Infantry Division which was coming in over the beaches.

Sicily was an important strategic objective. Not only would it offer airfields and staging areas as a stepping stone to the invasion of southern Europe, but it was also thought that the invasion of Sicily might expedite an Italian surrender. With the exception of raids by special forces troops, such as commandos, the parachute drop would allow the troopers of the 82nd Airborne to be among the very first allied troops to land in Europe.

Before launching the invasion, though, the Allies made many moves in the chess game they played with their Axis counterparts. The most famous of these ploys was probably Operation MINCEMEAT – better known as 'The Man Who Never Was' – in which a corpse supposedly carrying secret information regarding the invasion of Sardinia and Greece was planted on the German intelligence services. The top secret Ultra intercepts also proved important in the planning for Operation HUSKY. Ultra intercepts showed that two German armored units, the Hermann Goering Panzer Division and a Panzer Grenadier division were on Sicily stiffening the ten divisions of poor quality Italian troops garrisoning the island. However, the paratroopers were not informed of the presence of the Panzer units for fear that under interrogation if captured their knowledge might compromise the Ultra secret. As a result, the lightly-armed paratroopers were being sent in blind against German armored units.

Showing the initiative expected of paratroop officers, Col Gavin, two

A paratrooper of the 82nd Airborne stands in the door to illustrate proper jump techniques during training in North Africa prior to the jump on Sicily. (*US Army*)

of his battalion commanders and two pilots from the 52nd Troop Carrier Wing which would drop the paratroopers carried out a reconnaissance over Sicily in Mosquito bombers about a month before the jump. Heavy flak over Sicily prevented them getting a chance to recce the drop zones (DZs) in the Gela area, but they did reassure themselves that the pilots would be able to navigate to the DZs at night.

Enough intelligence was available from other sources to enable the troopers of the 82nd to lay out an exercise area in North Africa over terrain very similar to that near Gela. The DZ area was covered by sixteen key pill boxes which they would be expected to knock out. The 82nd carried out practice assaults on their exercise area against these objectives with live ammunition to prepare the paratroopers as thoroughly as possible for their impending mission. They would have to wait to find out what the target was.

British glider and parachute troops would also be taking part in the invasion of Sicily. As planning progressed, conflicts over the allocation of transport aircraft and other matters arose between Maj Gen Ridgway and the British airborne general 'Boy' Browning. The troopers who would be jumping into action were spared the conflicts of their superiors. They

Members of the 82nd Airborne give a mass demonstration jump at Oujda Airport in French Morocco during June 1943. (*US Army*)

were more concerned with surviving the heat and the dust of their training area. As soldiers have done throughout history, they speculated about where they would go into action. Sardinia, Greece, Sicily, Italy and France all had their advocates. At least a few men of the 82nd scoffed at such mundane targets and with the cockiness required of men who would jump into the unknown to face the enemy argued that they were going to jump over Berlin to assassinate Hitler!

On 5 July, although the paratroopers still had not been informed of their target, the ships carrying the invasion force sailed for Sicily. With the jump only days away, Ridgway continued to express concern about the fact that the planes carrying his men would be flying over the Allied invasion fleet at night, thus making them prey to jumpy sailors with their fingers on the triggers of anti-aircraft guns. Finally, on 7 July, the paratroopers were briefed that their objective was Sicily.

Early in the evening of 9 July, the troopers of the 505th Parachute Infantry and their comrades from the 504th and support units began to line up to board their aircraft. Shuffling under the weight of a hundred pounds or more of equipment the paratroopers anxiously awaited the orders to board their transport aircraft. Realizing that they might not receive

Members of the 505th Parachute Infantry board their aircraft for a training jump in North Africa during June 1943. (*US Army*)

resupply for some time, the large cargo pockets of their jump suits were crammed with grenades and they were festooned with extra bandoliers of ammunition. For most of the men this would be their first taste of combat, and they faced it with a mixture of anticipation and trepidation. The knowledge that they would be led by 'Slim Jim' Gavin helped calm them especially when they received a slip of paper just before takeoff bearing the following message from their highly respected commander:

Soldiers of the 505th Combat Team.

Tonight you embark upon a combat mission for which our people and the free people of the world have been waiting for two years.

You will spearhead the landing of an American Force upon the island of SICILY. Every preparation has been made to eliminate the element of chance. You have been given the means to do the job and you are backed by the largest assemblage of air power in the world's history.

The eyes of the world are upon you. The hopes and prayers of every American go with you . . .

James M. Gavin

Though perhaps not as colorful as the messages of George Patton, Gavin's low-key message proved inspiring to the tough paratroopers.

While 266 C-47s carried Gavin's paratroopers in nine-plane flights over the Mediterranean, glider-borne troops of the British 1st Airborne Division with the mission of seizing a bridge outside Syracuse were gaining the distinction of being the first Allied troops to land on Sicily. Though large numbers of gliders went into the sea or encountered other problems which kept them from their objective, a few Red Devils did manage to seize and hold the bridge, thus expediting Gen Montgomery's breakout from the invasion beachhead.

Meanwhile, the paratroopers of Gavin's 505th Parachute Regimental Team who would undertake 'Husky One,' as their mission was codenamed, were approaching their objective, though most of the transport pilots were lost. Having taken off not long after 20.00 hours, the C-47s had been flying for about three and a half hours on a complicated course and their pilots were relieved when they passed over the Sicilian coastline, even if they were not sure what part of the coastline they were crossing. The orders to the paratroopers had been to jump even under the most adverse conditions so, despite heavy winds which would have canceled a practice jump,

Member of the 82nd Airborne gains control of his chute during a practice jump in Morocco. (*US Army*)

Gavin in the lead C-47 was ready to precede his men out of the door. Also ready to jump with the regimental combat team was LTC 'Red' Ryder who had helped start the American airborne forces when he commanded the Parachute Test Platoon. Ryder was officially an observer, but Gavin intended to use him as a substitute battalion commander should one of his subordinates be killed or otherwise knocked out of the fight, a very likely possibility due to the aggressive leadership style of the paratroop officers.

To avoid detection, the transports had flown low over the Mediterranean, only gaining height as they approached the coast. The coast may have brought them close to their objective, but it also brought them under heavy anti-aircraft fire from the enemy which caused the already strung-out C-47s to scatter even more. As a result, virtually every stick of paratroopers was dropped off course.

The paratroopers' job was to jump, however, and as their planes approached what they thought was their drop zone, they went through the traditional paratroop litany before combat: 'Stand Up; Hook Up!' Throughout the armada of transport aircraft, this command was given by each plane's jumpmaster as more than 3,400 heavily-laden American paratroopers prepared to shuffle towards the door.

Good view of the 75mm pack howitzer being loaded aboard a Waco glider during training in North Africa prior to Operation Husky. (*US Army*)

Leaping immediately as the green light came on in his C-47, Col Gavin was the first American paratrooper on the ground, though what ground he was not sure! Soon, parachutes were blossoming all over southeastern Sicily. In some cases, the sticks were sent out of the door at only 300–400ft (90–120m) rather than the 700–800 (215–245m) expected jump altitude. This lower jump altitude along with the high winds and rocky terrain contributed to the substantial number of jump injuries incurred by the All Americans.

Injuries, scattering, darkness, and disorientation were all expected hazards during a night jump, however, and the paratroopers immediately began forming into groups using the name of the Army Chief of Staff as their passwords – sign: 'George', countersign: 'Marshall'. In some cases, as the paratroopers had hung suspended in their chutes, they had seen C-47s carrying some of their comrades shot down in flames. Soon after landing, most of the paratroopers realized they were out of their DZ, but it took some time to discover how far outside. In fact, the 505th Regimental Combat Team had been scattered over an area of 60 miles (100km).

As it turned out, only about one-eighth of the US paratroopers were dropped near their assigned DZs. Many of them were dropped in the British invasion area. There they created an unplanned diversion to help the British troops coming ashore, then fought on for days alongside the British infantrymen, though initially they had problems in linking up due to the use of a different password in the British section.

Throughout World War Two, US parachute assaults frequently consisted of dozens of small unit actions covering a wide area; this was exactly the case on Sicily. Paratroopers were trained to go onto the attack immediately whenever possible, creating maximum confusion in the enemy's rear. Among the first of the All Americans actually to engage the enemy were about eighty men of G Company, 505th Parachute Infantry, who were in a heavy firefight shortly after landing amidst the enemy defenders of Ponte Dirillo. Attacking ferociously, the paratroopers had soon cleared the well-entrenched German defenders from their pillboxes and seized a bridge necessary for the US 45th Infantry Division's breakout from its beachhead. The bridge had not been the company's objective, but it certainly proved a good substitute.

Other small groups of paratroopers cleared out German or Italian machine gun nests and other strongpoints as they encountered them. Even more importantly for confusing the island's defenders, they ambushed couriers and patrols and cut telephone lines thus inhibiting Axis communications when they were most needed to mount a cohesive counterthrust. In one action, fourteen paratroopers attacked and knocked out a group of pillboxes, capturing more than 250 Italians in the process.

One of the largest groups to land together was the bulk of the 2nd Battalion, 505th Parachute Infantry, though they were more than 20 miles (32km) from their assigned objective and right in the middle of a

Members of the 82nd Airborne lift the tail of a Waco glider prior to equipment being loaded aboard it. (*US Army*)

group of Italian strongpoints blocking the roads leading to the 45th Infantry's assigned beaches. Though his battalion was surrounded by strongly entrenched enemy troops, by morning Maj Mark Alexander's battalion had captured all the enemy positions – with fire support provided by a lone 75mm Pack Howitzer of the 456th Parachute Field Artillery – and had begun expanding their area of control. Although they too were way out of their assigned area, which was in the 1st Infantry Division zone, these paratroopers had taken aggressive action which would substantially assist the 45th Infantry in breaking out of their beachhead.

While the bulk of the regimental combat team had been attacking objectives of opportunity a long way from their assigned objectives, one of the few units to land near the combat team's objectives at Gela was Company I, 505th Parachute Infantry. Despite heavy odds, this small group of paratroopers managed to accomplish their mission, knocking out the Italian strongpoints and lighting bonfires to act as a beacon for the amphibious assault.

Elsewhere, about one hundred paratroopers of the 1st Battalion, 505th Parachute Infantry under LTC Arthur 'Hard Nose' Gorham had managed to seize and were holding much of the Objective Y area on Piano Lupo, the same area where the entire combat team was supposed to have landed. Gorham's troops soon faced an aggressive counterattack, which they fought off, knocking out four Italian tanks with bazookas in the process. It should be noted here that the bazooka was the only anti-tank weapon available to American paratroopers at this time, and it was not effective against heavy tanks and only marginally effective against medium tanks.

As might be expected, many of the scattered and/or injured paratroopers had been captured, but mistreatment of some American prisoners, such as one named Mike Scambelluri who would die from wounds sadistically inflicted piecemeal by an Italian officer on the bound paratrooper, caused tough paratroopers quickly to develop a no-quarter attitude, especially with the Italians.

Just as their comrades who found themselves in the 45th Infantry Division area had attacked targets of opportunity, so did those members of the 505th Combat Team who found themselves in the British invasion area take advantage of their position in the enemy rear to create maximum confusion. Seventy-five paratroopers, for example, attacked the town of Avola, where they linked up with British infantrymen advancing out of the beachhead, though at first the British fired on them thinking they were

Members of Battery A, 320th Airborne Field Artillery aboard their glider along with their 75mm pack howitzer. (*US Army*)

Airborne artillerymen of the 82nd Airborne preparing to lash down their 75mm pack howitzer aboard a Waco glider. Note that the wartime censor has obliterated their shoulder insignia. (*US Army*)

Germans. This reaction was, of course, understandable since no Americans were supposed to be within miles. Still, the British felt the paratroopers had lent very valuable assistance in seizing Avola.

Throughout the early hours of the invasion, Col Gavin had found himself separated from most of his command; in fact, he did not link up with substantial numbers of his men until D+1 when he finally managed to round up about two hundred and fifty paratroopers, mostly from the 3rd Battalion, 505th Parachute Infantry. Anxious for action and realizing the importance of seizing the high ground overlooking the 45th Infantry Division's positions, Gavin led his men in an assault on German positions on the high ground, successfully driving off the Germans. Gavin did not realize they were from the Hermann Goering Fallschirmpanzer Division, and led his paratroopers in pursuit only to run into heavy Tiger tanks. Against the massive Tigers, the bazookas of the All Americans proved ineffective as the rounds just bounced off. However, a 75mm pack howitzer from the 456th Parachute Field Artillery used in the direct fire mode did manage temporarily to drive off the huge German tanks. Later German counterattacks were diffused, thanks to the tenacity of the All Americans and to heavy artillery support from 155mm artillery of the 45th Infantry Division and naval gunfire support. The paratroopers had held the high ground but had suffered heavy casualties in the process.

Though far from their assigned objectives, in fact, the troopers of the 82nd Airborne had fortuitously dropped between the Hermann Goering Panzer Division and the invasion beaches, thus buying the amphibious assault troops time to come ashore and consolidate. Men of the 505th Regimental Combat Team soon helped the US 1st Infantry Division to fight off German counterattacks, thus preparing the ground for the breakout of Patton's Seventh Army and the drive up the coast of Sicily.

The 3rd Battalion, 504th Parachute Infantry, the lone representatives of their regiment to jump with the combat team, managed to tie down other elements of the Hermann Goering Division as they captured two Italian 57mm anti-tank guns and dug in along the Niscemi-Biscari Highway. Using their captured anti-tank guns and mines which they had planted along the road, they managed to drive off an advancing German column. Other small groups of parachutists hit other Hermann Goering columns, slowing the Germans' counterattack even more. One company of the 504th

Good view of the nose of a Waco glider lifted while members of the 82nd Airborne board a jeep. (*US Army*)

seized a castle on the northern Piano Lupo and held it against repeat-ed German counterattacks which might otherwise have been directed against the beachhead until D+3 when they were finally relieved by the 1st Infantry Division.

As with future airborne operations, 'Husky One' illustrated the impor-tance of aggressiveness and initiative on the part of paratroopers. Despite the scattered drops, the All Americans had acted decisively to create mas-sive confusion in the enemy rear, while just a couple of hundred of them had still managed to secure all of the objectives assigned to the entire regimental combat team. As a result, the other small attacks taking place all over southeastern Sicily had been a bonus which augmented the diffi-culties faced by the defenders in countering the Allied landings. So much confusion had the 3,400 paratroopers created, in fact, that the defenders thought they were dealing with three or four airborne divisions and it was even announced over the radio in Rome that Sicily was being invaded by five or more Allied airborne divisions.

Though he was still extremely worried about the danger of trigger-happy army and navy anti-aircraft gunners shooting down the drop planes, which would be sitting ducks as they approached the drop zone, Ridgway ordered his second wave to jump on the evening of D+1. It comprised the rest of the 504th Parachute Infantry, the 376th Parachute Artillery, and the rest of the 307th Parachute Engineer Battalion. Commanding the 2nd battalion of the 504th on this jump would be LTC William Yarborough, the designer of the parachutists' wings and jump boots.

After the flight from North Africa, the first C-47s arrived over their DZ at Farello airfield without incident and dropped their sticks right on target. However, after one American anti-aircraft gunner opened up by mistake on the C-47s of the second wave, a hail of machine gun and cannon fire engulfed the vulnerable transport aircraft. Aircrew and paratroopers died in their hundreds as twenty-three out of the 144 C-47s were shot down in flames or exploded, while many others were severely damaged. The panicked gunners, who were supposed to be aware of the follow-up parachute drop, thought they were firing at German bombers. To com-pound the disaster, they kept shooting at aircraft which had successfully ditched in the sea or at paratroopers descending to the ground in the belief that they were German parachutists. By the time this fire disaster had ended, 318 aircrew and paratroopers had been killed, including Brig Gen Charles Keerans, the 82nd's Assistant Division Commander, who had gone along as an observer. The number of severely injured was also well into the hundreds, many of them aboard transports which had limped back to North Africa rather than attempt to drop their sticks into what appeared to be a shrapnel-filled hell. So heavy was the carnage, in fact, that almost twenty-four hours after the jump only a little over twenty-five per cent of the paratroopers who had set out from North Africa were on the airfield with the regimental commander Rueben Tucker.

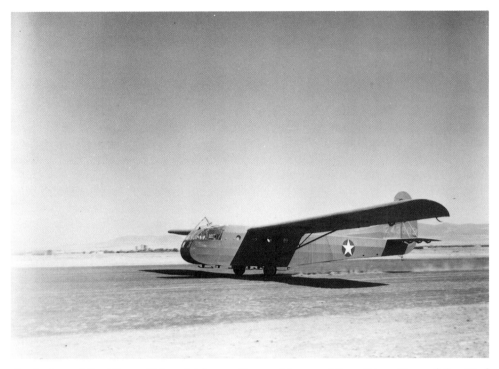

Good view of the Waco glider which was the workhorse of the glider riders of the 82nd Airborne. (*US Army*)

Two nights later, on 13 July, the British were to make a jump to seize the Primasole bridge in Operation FUSTION, the final airborne phase of the Sicily invasion. Ironically, German paratroopers jumped into the same DZ to reinforce the defenders only minutes ahead of the assault by the Red Devils, but the tough British paratroopers managed to rout their surprised German equivalents after a hard close quarters battle.

Once the Allied beachhead had been firmly established, Maj Gen Ridgway, who had come in over the beach, took command of the 82nd Airborne elements, which were withdrawn and augmented with heavier artillery units. The 82nd then served as 'leg' infantry with Patton's 7th Army for the remainder of the Sicilian campaign. Because of the heavy casualties suffered during the airborne assault and the need to save the highly trained paratroopers for future jumps, Patton did not assign them the toughest missions. However, the All Americans did get a chance to see further combat. During one phase of the advance, LTC Yarborough, carrying out a recce miles ahead of the rest of his battalion, took over one hundred Italians prisoner with the assistance of just two other paratroopers. Showing the ferocity for which American paratroopers would become famous during the war, another All American officer led his platoon in a bayonet charge to

seize Tumminello Pass, which routed the Italian defenders. The 82nd also
helped to solve the critical problem of port facilities when they captured
the port of Trapini along with five thousand prisoners.

In the after action analysis of the Sicilian campaign, there were many
debits against the parachute assault. The widely scattered drops and the
friendly fire fiasco heavily influenced Gen Eisenhower to recommend
that the airborne divisions be broken up and that in the future they
only be used in regimental strength. On the plus side, all had to admit
that the All Americans had shown a tenacious and aggressive fighting
spirit which could not be faulted. Despite Eisenhower's criticisms, Lt Gen
George Patton, probably the best judge of fighting men in the US Army,
believed that the paratroopers had speeded his breakout by at least forty-
eight hours. Gen Kurt Student, admittedly a somewhat biased advocate
of paratroopers, since he commanded German parachute forces, believed
that had the men of the 82nd Airborne not been in blocking positions
between the Hermann Goering Division and the beaches the US assault
might have been repulsed.

Eisenhower ordered an investigation into the shooting down of the

In July 1943, after jumping into Sicily, the commander of the 82nd, Maj Gen Matthew
Ridgway along with members of his staff overlooking the battlefield near Riberia, Sicily.
(*US Army*)

transport aircraft by friendly anti-aircraft fire, but obviously no one was willing to admit blame and there were so many conflicting statements that it was impossible to lay the blame on any one individual or unit. The closest the investigators came to a consensus was that the flight plan had been faulty since it carried the flight along 35 miles of beaches filled with green troops who had already been subjected to German bomber attacks which had increased their anxiety. Though no final blame was laid, for some time it would have been ill-advised for someone to introduce himself to one of the tough All Americans as a naval or army anti-aircraft gunner who had been at Sicily.

Acting on Eisenhower's recommendation that the airborne divisions be broken up, Gen Marshall established the Swing Board, under the commander of the 11th Airborne Division, to make recommendations for improved effectiveness in future airborne operations. Among the resulting changes were a more clearly defined command relationship between the airborne forces and Troop Carrier Command and the establishment of Air Corps and Army airborne pathfinder units. The pathfinders would consist of experienced pilots and ten-man teams of paratroopers. The pilots would navigate their aircraft to the drop zones about twenty minutes ahead of the main assault force and drop the pathfinder teams who would set up lights and electronic homing devices to aid the main assault force in identifying the drop zone.

Though the 82nd Airborne's first leap into combat on Sicily had been beset with obvious problems, the All Americans had certainly proved their ability to fight. They could not guarantee that the Air Corps would not drop them off course or that anti-aircraft gunners would not shoot them down. All they could do was guarantee that they would make things difficult for any enemy they found themselves near once they hit the ground. On Sicily they did this with a vengeance.

4   TARGET: ROME

After the successful invasion of Sicily, the Italians seemed even more willing to negotiate a separate peace. Realizing the importance of pushing Italy out of the war, the Combined Chiefs of Staff approved the invasion of the Italian mainland on 20 July 1943. The Italian will to fight suffered another blow on 24 July when Mussolini was replaced after more than two decades in power by Marshal Badoglio. Distrustful of Italy's continued combat effectiveness, Hitler now committed additional German troops to Italy. Though the presence of the more combat effective German divisions would increase the difficulties in invading the Italian mainland, they would also be further away from the beaches in northern France when the time came for the invasion across the Channel.

Plans were formulated for an amphibious assault on the Italian mainland. Salerno was the principal objective (Operation AVALANCHE), though a supporting invasion of the toe and heel of the Italian boot would be launched by Montgomery's 8th Army, with Foggia and the surrounding airfields as prime objectives (Operations BUTTRESS and BAYTOWN). Following Montgomery's opening assault, Mark Clark's 5th US Army would invade at Salerno on 9 September and then drive north to capture Naples. In support of these amphibious landings, the 82nd Airborne's regimental commanders were told on 1 August to plan for a parachute and glider assault. Their primary objective would be Sorrento Ridge, the important high ground overlooking the invasion beaches and the plain leading to Naples. In addition to seizing the high ground, the airborne troops would take and hold the passes leading northwest from Salerno.

As Ridgway's staff were finalizing their plans for this operation, it was canceled in favour of a parachute jump combined with an amphibious assault to seize the key bridges crossing the Volturno River, destroying them if necessary to block a German counterattack against the invasion forces coming over the beaches. According to the plan, the 504th and 505th Parachute Infantry Regiments would jump on the banks of the river to secure the bridges while the 325th Glider Infantry came in from the sea. Based on the bazooka's inability to deal with German Tiger tanks on Sicily, 57mm anti-tank guns had been added to the armament of the glider artillery. During the planning stages, the possibility that the 82nd would be surrounded for days until conventional units linked up dictated that aerial resupply became a prime consideration.

On 20 August, the 82nd was withdrawn to North Africa where the

Paratroopers of the 82nd Airborne Division don their chutes in North Africa prior to the Salerno jump. (*US Army*)

division began preparing for GIANT ONE, as the jump against the Volturna River bridges was codenamed. Since intelligence indicated that in addition to their old enemies from Sicily, the Hermann Goering Fallschirmpanzer Division, they would be going up against the German 1st Fallschirmjäger (parachute) Division, the All Americans were anticipating seeing how good their German counterparts were.

Due to lessons learned from the Sicily jump, much thought was devoted to correcting the problems encountered in delivering the sticks to the drop zones at night. The pathfinder units, whose formation has already been mentioned, trained intensively in preparation for their first combat jump, experimenting with the small Rebecca-Eureka radar set and Krypton lights which would be used to guide in the C-47s carrying the assault force.

In the meantime, as the men of the 82nd trained for their next combat jump, Giuseppe Castellano, an Italian general, contacted the Allies to tell them that the Italians would change sides and help the Allies fight the Germans. However, to satisfy Italian honor, an Allied landing would first have to be made on the mainland. The Italians' primary fear was that the Italian troops garrisoning Rome would be unable to prevent the Germans from seizing the city as soon as Badoglio announced the armistice with the Allies. Therefore, Castellano requested that the Allies drop a division of paratroopers on Rome and drive an armored division up the Tiber to link up with the paratroopers, thus securing the Eternal City. Since the 82nd would be tabbed for this mission should it come off, on 31 August, 'GIANT ONE' was canceled. Then Ridgway was ordered to begin planning for an 8 September drop on Rome, after which the All Americans would link up with the Italian troops and hold Rome until relieved by advancing American troops.

Based on intelligence supplied by Italian officers on the disposition of German troops around Rome, Ridgway's staff planned a combined parachute, airlanding and amphibious assault on Rome. This operation would be codenamed GIANT TWO. According to the plan, on 8 September at 18.30 hours, Eisenhower would announce the invasion and armistice over the radio. Simultaneously, the 504th Parachute Infantry Regiment would take off to drop and seize Cerveteri and Furbara airfields. The next night, the 505th Parachute Infantry Regiment would jump on Littoria, Glidonia and Centocelle airfields. Once the airfields were secured, the 325th Glider Infantry would be airlanded from C-47s. To lend heavier firepower, on the night of 9 September, the 319th Glider Field Artillery, the 80th Airborne Anti-Aircraft Battalion and attached tank destroyer units would make an amphibious landing and drive to link up with their comrades. Italian troops would provide navigational aids, guides, interpreters and ground transport for the paratroopers.

Though he continued with the plans as ordered, Ridgway felt that even with Italian assistance – assistance, it should be noted, whose reliability was somewhat questionable – the heavy concentration of German anti-aircraft guns around Rome made the plan dangerous. Still, the seizure of

Layout of airborne equipment gives some idea of the heavy load members of the 82nd jumped with. The machete would not normally be used in Europe, but the Thompson SMG, 1911 pistol, grenades, fighting knife, etc. would help arm the American paratroopers. The layout also includes demolition charges in the upper center between the main and reserve chutes. (*US Army*)

Rome was at this point viewed as so important that Ridgway was ordered to continue planning for the operation. In preparation for the operation, on 4 and 5 September, the 82nd was deployed to Sicily from where the operation would be launched.

Eisenhower himself soon became skeptical about the operation's viability; hence, he decided to send in Brig Gen Maxwell Taylor of the 82nd and an Air Force colonel to carry out a personal reconnaissance inside Rome. Taylor was given full authority to call off GIANT TWO by transmitting a single codeword should he not be convinced the operation would work. Smuggled into Rome, Taylor, in full US Army uniform, met with Italian officers. Then in a personal meeting with Marshal Badoglio, he learned that the Germans had increased their presence around Rome, as a result of which the Italians were backing out of their agreement at the eleventh hour.

As a result of this meeting, he sent a message explaining the situation but not actually calling off GIANT TWO. Eisenhower received the message just after 08.00 hours on 8 September while the 504th Parachute Infantry were already preparing for their jump. Then, at 11.35 hours, Taylor sent the coded message calling off the operation. Eisenhower did not want to rely on the radio for the abort command and sent a personal messenger by plane. The messenger, however, was delayed in landing at Sicily until after the first sticks of the 504th had already taken off. Sixty-two plane loads of All Americans who were already winging their way to Rome had to be called back. Whether the mission would have succeeded as a classic coup de main or whether it would have been the sacrifice of the entire 82nd has been debated ever since it was canceled. Airborne theorists felt that it would have been a classic vertical envelopment, but James Gavin, at the time the commander of the 505th Parachute Infantry and later of the entire division, walked over the planned drop zones in 1950 and concluded that Taylor was absolutely correct in aborting the mission.

One aspect of GIANT TWO did take place as planned through an oversight. A small raiding force of forty-six men from the 509th Parachute Infantry, the proud veterans of the North African jumps who were still attached·to the 82nd, had been assigned the mission of knocking out a German radar station on the island of Ventotene to prevent the radar detecting the armada of transports on the way to Rome. In addition to blowing up the radar station successfully, half of the raiders – twenty-three paratroopers – managed to capture 115 Germans. When the Germans realized how small the raiding force was, they regretted their surrender, but twenty-three tough-looking paratroopers armed with Thompson SMGs convinced them to stay docile.

At 03.30 hours on 9 September, the 5th Army carried out their landings at Salerno without airborne assistance. However, the cancelation of the parachute jump on the heights overlooking the beaches proved hazardous for the invasion force as the Germans used the heights as a pivot from which to launch vigorous counterattacks against the beachhead. So vigorous, in fact, was the German counterstroke that Mark Clark sent a personal message to Ridgway on the morning of 13 September asking for immediate reinforcements to jump directly into the beachhead. As soon as Ridgway received the message, he ordered his regimental commanders into action and a plan was ready by 18.30 hours. By 19.30 hours, battalions of the 504th Parachute Infantry Regiment were already taking off for Salerno. The pathfinders went in first. To assist the pathfinders in guiding in the 504th, Clark's ground troops also built a fiery 'T' as a marker. To avoid drift and keep the landings tight, the All Americans would bail out at only 600ft (180m) cutting hang time to a minimum. With the exception of one company which was dropped 10 miles (16km) off course, the rest of the 504th were right on the drop zone.

Meanwhile, due to the critical situation on the beachhead, the 509th Parachute Infantry Battalion, which was still attached to the 82nd, was

Members of the 82nd Airborne Division prepare in September 1943 for the Salerno jump. (*US Army*)

ordered to drop 16 miles inland at Avellino to seize the key junction of three highways. By interdicting road traffic at Avellino, the 509th would be able to impede the flow of German reinforcements to both Salerno and Naples. Because mountains surrounded the town, the 509th would be jumping from over 4,000ft (1,220m), making this the highest altitude combat jump of the war. Like the 504th Parachute Infantry, the 509th was alerted to their mission with little notice, being ordered on the afternoon of 13 September to prepare to jump that evening. Their orders were to seize and hold Avellino until relieved by the 5th Army; if the battalion could not accomplish this mission, they were ordered to create maximum havoc in the German rear to tie down as many Germans as possible and harass lines of communication.

At 21.00 hours on 13 September, the small pathfinder detachment assigned to leap in ahead of the 509th took off; however, the radar beacon emplaced by the pathfinders was blocked by the surrounding mountains, causing the flight bearing the paratroopers to become scattered, only about ten out of forty sticks dropping on the Avellino DZs. So badly scattered was the 509th, in fact, that the seizure of Avellino, which had been garrisoned by German armored troops, became impossible. A substantial number of 509th troopers were taken prisoner, including LTC Doyle Yardley, the battalion CO; nevertheless, groups of 509th paratroopers began cutting German telephone lines, ambushing German columns, blowing bridges and ambushing messengers. At least one group of paratroopers linked up with Italian partisans and carried out operations with them.

Although Mark Clark's 5th Army headquarters could not establish radio communications with the 509th and assumed the battalion had been eliminated, the scattered paratroopers were doing a very effective job of distracting German attention from the beachhead as they tied down more and more of the Wehrmacht on anti-paratrooper operations. When advancing British units assigned to the 5th Army finally linked up with the paratroopers of the 509th, they acted as scouts for the British. By the time the 5th Army linked up with the 509th, however, the paratroopers had suffered more than one-third casualties.

Further to reinforce the beachhead, the 505th had jumped in on the night of 14 September, right on target despite the fact that the fiery 'T' was not lit until the jumpers had already hit the silk. The combination of the tough reputation of the paratroopers and the drama of their jump into the beachhead was a shot in the arm for the 'legs' pinned down in the beachhead. Catching some of the aggressive spirit of the All Americans, they held off the German counterattacks and consolidated their foothold on the Italian mainland.

The beaches fully secured, on 15 September the 325th Glider Infantry along with one battalion of the 504th Parachute Infantry landed from the sea. Shortly, the newly arrived battalion, Reuben Tucker's 504th, captured Hill 424, a key objective, on 16 September, and held it against

Brig Gen Gavin, who always jumped into combat with the lead sticks of the 82nd, checks his equipment prior to emplaning for Operation Market Garden. (*US Army*)

heavy German counterattacks the next morning. When given permission to withdraw, in fact, Tucker replied 'Retreat hell! – Send me my other battalion!' The battalion was sent to rejoin Tucker's regiment which held until relieved. During the battle, the paratroopers suffered heavy casualties, totalling 181, but inflicted up to four times as many casualties on the enemy.

Once the threat to the beachhead had been countered, the 82nd Airborne moved to Amalfi. The 505th Parachute Infantry got the distinction of capturing Pompeii and then, attached to the British 23rd Armoured Division, leading the entry into Naples. With Naples secured, the 82nd drew the task of policing the city, which often meant that paratroopers who understood virtually no Italian found themselves being called upon to settle minor domestic disputes. Between 3 and 9 October, the members of Gavin's 505th were back in action as they helped to clear the Germans from the banks of the Volturno River and then became the first Allied unit to cross the river. Shortly after this crossing the 505th got a new commander as Gavin was promoted to the rank of brigadier general and made Assistant Division Commander. His successor was Col Herbert Batcheller.

As the US 5th Army and British 8th Army advanced, the 504th

Parachute Infantry was assigned the critical mission of filling a gap between the two armies. The 504th, as a result, found itself fighting in the mountains until late December. The combination of the innate toughness of the paratroopers, their ability to fight without heavy support and their skill at small unit actions made them extremely effective in the mountains, as they severely punished the Germans facing them, though once again at the cost of heavy casualties to the 504th.

When the 504th was finally pulled back, it was not to rest but to prepare for another mission, a parachute jump behind the Anzio beachhead, but the parachute jump was canceled and the 504th went in over the beaches instead. Intended to bypass the German Gothic Line defenses and drive through a rapid advance on Rome, the Anzio beachhead soon turned into a pocket eventually containing seven Allied divisions. Initially, the 504th was held in reserve, but on 22 January they were sent in under the 3rd Infantry Division to bolster the right flank. Augmenting the 504th, which was, in effect, a regimental combat team, were the 376th Parachute Artillery and Company C, 307th Parachute Engineers.

Offense was more to the paratroopers' taste than defense and, on 24 January, after heavy fighting, the 504th seized positions along the Mussolini Canal. It was along this canal, too, that the 504th won their nickname – 'The Devils in Baggy Pants' – from the description a German officer had written of them in his diary.

One battalion, the 3/504th, was later heavily engaged on the defensive at Aprilia where they held off repeated German counterattacks between 8 and 12 February, managing to rescue a British general from the Germans in the process. Though suffering extremely heavy casualties, the tough paratroopers proved tenacious defenders, winning a Presidential Unit Citation for their courageous defense.

After the 509th Parachute Infantry Battalion had been pulled back following their jump at Avellino, they acted as the HQ guard unit for 5th Army under their new CO, LTC William Yarborough. Yarborough, who had already created the parachute badge and jump boots, started another airborne tradition as commander of the 509th when he instituted the practice of wearing small stars representing each combat jump on the parachute wings. Eventually, this practice became standard throughout the airborne forces. Like the 504th, the 509th was ordered to take part in the Anzio landings, going in with the initial assault forces and occupying the town of Nettuno, 2 miles (3.2 km) east of Anzio. On 8 February, as the 509th was defending near the town of Carano, Corporal Paul Huff won the first Congressional Medal of Honor awarded to a paratrooper as he routed 125 Germans virtually single-handed. The 509th continued to see action, seventy-three straight days of combat, in fact, before being withdrawn from the beachhead in late March after once again suffering extremely heavy casualties. The 509th now parted company with the

82nd Airborne as the All Americans were preparing for the invasion of the north of France while the 509th was slated to see action in the invasion of the south of France.

Before the 504th was even committed at Anzio, the remainder of the 82nd was pulled out of combat and continued training and evaluating the experience gained in their latest operational jump. Pathfinders had proved invaluable when jumping at Salerno, but attempts were made to improve the effectiveness of the pathfinders even further. Special emphasis was given to guiding in gliders at night. Based on the experiences during the Sicily jump, the aggressive doctrine which held that paratroopers would immediately attack any enemy encountered after landing was re-evaluated. The resulting change in doctrine did not seek to blunt the aggressive combat effectiveness of the All Americans but did stress that when faced with overwhelming force there were times when the paratroopers should avoid combat in order to infiltrate to their objective. No matter what their objective, the traditional airborne secondary objective remained to create as much confusion as possible in the enemy rear. As assistant division commander, Brig Gen Gavin had left for London to

Another layout of equipment, this time for a mortarman, who will jump with the tripod to his team's mortar. Note that instead of a Thompson SMG he is equipped with a Garand rifle. Later in the war, especially, the M1A1 carbine became widely used among paratroopers instead of the heavier Garand or Thompson. (*US Army*)

act as the chief airborne planner for the Normandy invasion. Beginning in November 1943, then, the lead elements of the 82nd began leaving for Great Britain in preparation for Operation OVERLORD as well.

Having helped blunt the German thrust to throw the Allies off the Anzio beachhead, the 504th was used in defensive positions for the next few weeks until being pulled out on 23 March, though the Allies would not break out of the beachhead until two months later. During their time at Anzio, the 504th Parachute Infantry Regiment, which had already been depleted by losses around Salerno, suffered 590 more casualties, but once again had inflicted far more casualties on the Germans. The next stop for the 504th was Great Britain where they arrived on 10 April 1944 to rejoin the remainder of the division.

With two operational parachute jumps under its belt, the 82nd Airborne Division was now ready to prepare for the most ambitious airborne operation in the war so far.

5 BREACHING HITLER'S ATLANTIC WALL

Heavily laden 82nd Airborne paratrooper boards his transport prior to the jump over Normandy. Note that he is armed with the M1 Thompson SMG. (*IWM*)

As the planning for Operation OVERLORD, the Allied cross-channel invasion of France, progressed, All American Assistant Division Commander
Gavin often found that dealing with political infighting was just as difficult
as dealing with Tiger tanks had been on Sicily. Particular problems were
encountered with Lt Gen 'Boy' Browning, the British airborne general, who
was constantly fighting to exert British control over American airborne
forces. It should be noted, however, that such struggles for 'turf' at the top
had little adverse effect on the relationship between British and American
paratroopers at the troop levels. American and British paratroopers still
respected each other for their shared 'exits from a plane in flight' and,
though the cockiness of the American paratroopers and their far superi-
or jump pay may at times have rubbed the Red Devils the wrong way,
the tens of thousands of Allied paratroopers stationed near each other in
England prior to the massive Normandy jump got on surprisingly well,
especially considering that aggressiveness was something of a prerequisite
for the airborne forces.

During the planning stages, the airborne phase of OVERLORD underwent
many changes. Initially, the American airborne phase was envisaged as
company and battalion-sized jumps just behind the invasion beaches to
neutralize the German shore batteries. At another point, it was suggested
that most of the 82nd and 101st Airborne Divisions – the two US airborne
units earmarked for OVERLORD – would come in over the beaches as
amphibious assault troops. Omar Bradley, who was commanding the US
assault force, however, was a great supporter of the airborne troops and
insisted that they be dropped inland to help ensure the success of his landings. As a result, in late December 1943, Gavin was called into Bradley's
office to discuss possible DZs for the parachute landings.

To help the 101st Airborne benefit from the 82nd's combat experience
in Sicily and Italy, Gavin was also charged with standardizing practices
among the American airborne forces which would take part in the invasion.
Nevertheless, Gavin was anxious to leave his staff position and rejoin the
All Americans, which he did on 6 February 1944. The 82nd had originally
landed in Northern Ireland, but when Gavin rejoined them they had moved
to Leicester where they were resting from their blooding in Sicily and Italy
and were training for the upcoming invasion of France. With the initiative
expected of paratroopers, the men of the 82nd still found enough time to get
to know many local English girls and to become familiar with the local public
houses. Among those remembered with particularly fond memories by the
All Americans were 'The Queens,' 'The Royal Oak', 'The Swan with Two
Heads' and 'The Haunch of Venison' where boxing matches were arranged
between 82nd pugilists and those from the British airborne forces.

The 504th Parachute Infantry Regiment finally rejoined the division
in May 1944, after its service in Anzio. However, due to its depleted state
it was not expected to take part in the invasion of France, and two new
regiments had been assigned to the 82nd in January 1944, the 507th and

508th Parachute Infantry. To help to replace the casualties the 504th and other units had suffered in Sicily and Italy, the 82nd established a jump school at Leicester. While at Leicester, the men of the 325th Glider Infantry and the other glider riders came closer to receiving parity with their parachute brethren as they received a pay increase and were allowed to wear their own glider wings.

Initially, the 82nd's mission in Normandy was broken down as follows: the 505th Parachute Infantry would land behind Utah Beach in the area west of St Sauveur-le-Vicomte and seize the town and nearby bridges over the Douve River; the 507th Parachute Infantry would land north of the rest of the division and protect the flank; and the 508th Parachute Infantry would land on Hill 110, then block German reinforcements. The indications were that Hill 110 could be the toughest objective, especially since aerial photographs indicated that the Germans were building anti-paratroop obstacles known as *Rommelspargel* (Rommel's asparagus), consisting of poles linked by wires attached to mines, and moving reinforcements into the area. According to this initial plan, the airborne forces would carry out daylight landings beginning at about 09.00 hours on D-Day.

As the plan evolved, 82nd Airborne staff officers carefully scrutinized aerial photographs for changes in the German defenses. Meanwhile there was a great deal of activity in February 1944 as a plan was suggested from Washington which called for the seizure of a giant airhead around Paris by three airborne divisions which would then hold the French capital until relieved by the forces advancing over the beaches. Eisenhower did, however, manage to convince the Combined Chiefs that this plan could well mean the sacrifice of the three divisions should the German defense prove tenacious on the beaches. Without the airborne forces dropping near the beaches, too, even gaining a foothold on the French coast let alone driving towards Paris could prove extremely difficult.

February also saw the augmentation of the glider forces for the impending invasion. The 82nd's 325th Glider Infantry, for example, was given an additional battalion. By February, too, 2,100 Waco CG-4A gliders had arrived in Great Britain for use in the airborne operations, though not all had been assembled as there was a shortage of skilled labor.

The toughening of German defenses under Field Marshal Rommel caused a revision of the airborne plan which called for the 82nd's drop zones to move 10 miles (16km) east of St-Sauveur-le-Vicomte. Just as the 82nd's regimental commanders were finalizing plans for their new objectives, however, there was a final change on 26 May, less than two weeks before the jump. This final plan moved the drop zones for the 82nd and 101st Airborne Divisions closer to each other thus minimizing the possibility of the two divisions being cut off behind German lines without support. Under the final plan, the airborne units would go in at about 01.00 hours on D-Day, hours before the amphibious assault.

The 82nd's new mission called for landings on both sides of the Merderet

River. The All Americans would then seize and hold Neuville-au-Plain, Ste Mère-Eglise, Chef du Pont, Etienville and Amfreville and their surrounding areas. The crossings over the Douve River were to be destroyed to prevent the Germans from reinforcing their defenses along the beachhead. Ironically, Ste Mère-Eglise, which would become legendary for the All Americans, had initially been a 101st Airborne objective and was assigned to the 82nd during the final revision of the airborne assault plan. Unfortunately, aerial photographs did not indicate the extreme marshiness of the ground around the Merderet and Douve Rivers.

The operational plan called for the 82nd's paratroopers to jump into three DZs while All American glider riders would go into one landing zone (LZ). The 82nd's new regiments, the 507th and 508th Parachute Infantry, would jump near the west bank of the Merderet River and establish defensive positions to seal off the Cotentin Peninsula. The veteran 505th Parachute Infantry would jump east of the Merderet and capture two bridges across the river as well as Ste Mère-Eglise to interdict the main road passing through the town. The 325th Glider Infantry would also land on the east side of the Merderet and act as a reserve to be committed as needed.

Under Edson D. Raff, some members of the 325th Glider Infantry and a portion of the 82nd's Glider Field Artillery would come in over the beaches. Their mission was to drive inland as fast as possible to link up with the remainder of the division. This use of a portion of the 82nd as amphibious rather than airborne troops resulted from the shortage of glider pilots, a shortage which also resulted in paratroopers acting as co-pilots aboard gliders during the Normandy operation.

Paratroopers of the 82nd were on their airfields ready to go on 4 June because the drop was initially scheduled for shortly after midnight on 5 June, but the invasion was postponed for a day due to bad weather. Though the weather remained bad, on the afternoon of 5 June, the All Americans prepared for action, checking their equipment and chutes. Realizing they were likely to see heavy combat after landing, the airborne troopers were heavily armed. Typical individual weapons might include an M1 rifle, 156 rounds of ammunition, a .45 pistol with three magazines of ammunition, four grenades and a fighting knife. Typically, the grenades were stuffed into the large cargo pockets on the jump suit, a practice which led to disaster for thirteen members of the HQ company of the 1st Battalion, 505th Parachute Infantry. As they prepared to board their C-47, a grenade carried by one of the men exploded, killing three men and wounding ten and doing extensive damage to the aircraft.

When the 378 transport aircraft carrying the 82nd's three parachute regiments took off, they would fly at 500ft (150m) until nearing the French coast, at which point they would climb to 1,500ft (460m) to avoid the coastal defenses, then drop to 500ft (150m) to disgorge their sticks of paratroopers. Along with the paratroopers would be fifty-two gliders carrying heavy equipment such as anti-tank guns.

Most of the 82nd's glider troops would, however, land during the night of D+1.

At about 23.00 hours on 5 June 1944, the pathfinders for the largest airborne assault in history began taking off. Not long after midnight, they were followed by the main assault force carried in over one thousand C-47s. The first pathfinders from the 82nd touched down on French soil at about 01.21 hours on 6 June. Many of the 82nd's pathfinders had been dropped off course, and, therefore, many did not turn on their homing devices either from fear of drawing the main assault force off course or due to the nearness of enemy troops.

The three All American parachute regiments under the direct command of Brig Gen Gavin faced problems of scattering as well. The lack of pathfinders combined with heavy anti-aircraft fire which caused the pilots to veer off course contributed to the scattering problem, while the hedgerows in Normandy made assembling the scattered paratroopers more difficult than usual. The fact that many paratroopers landed amidst marshes which bogged down their progress or swallowed their equipment magnified the problems of assembling a cohesive fighting force even more. Actually, the 82nd suffered worse from scattered drops than the 101st since the Screaming Eagles had crossed the coast first thus alerting the anti-aircraft gunners to the transports which followed carrying the All Americans.

As it turned out, only the 505th Parachute Infantry were dropped near their assigned DZ. The 3/505th hastily assembled and drove on to seize their objective, the village of Ste Mère-Eglise, before dawn, though they were horrified to find many dead comrades who had landed in the town and been shot by the Germans. The unit's CO, LTC Krause, quickly marked the liberation of the town by raising the stars and stripes, the same flag, in fact, which the regiment had raised upon liberating Naples. At 09.30 hours on 6 June, the expected German counterattack, supported by tanks, hit the 3/505th.

The 2/505th, which had been advancing on its objective at Neuville-au-Plain, was ordered to reinforce Ste Mère-Eglise. However, LTC Vandervoort, the 2/505th CO, made an important tactical decision when he sent one reinforced rifle platoon of forty-eight men under Lt Turner Turnbull to set up a blocking position at Neuville-au-Plain, to interdict German reinforcements moving towards Ste Mère-Eglise. As it turned out, Vandervoort's decision was very critical as the blocking force at Neuville-au-Plain held a far superior German force at bay for four hours, suffering twenty per cent casualties in the process. Fortunately, one of the few 57mm anti-tank guns to survive the glider landings in Normandy was available at Neuville-au-Plain to lend firepower to Turnbull's outnumbered band. Their stand plus the heroic defense of Ste Mère-Eglise by Krause's 3rd Battalion, augmented by strays from other regiments who had drifted in, stalled the German counterattack towards the beaches. The paratroopers were reinforced on the night of 6 June

82nd Airborne trooper shares a drink with a captured German medic after the night jump over Normandy. (*IWM*)

when glider infantrymen of the 325th Glider Infantry and glider artillery joined them.

The remaining battalion of the 505th, the 1st, had the mission of securing the bridge at la Fière over the Merderet River but ran into heavy German resistance, unsuccessfully assaulting three times at the cost of heavy casualties.

Brig Gen Gavin himself had jumped about three miles off course, but he eventually managed to round up about five hundred assorted paratroopers. Half of them were sent to help seize the la Fière bridgehead and the other half were sent to take the Chef du Pont bridgehead. The village of Chef du Pont was successfully taken as was the eastern end of the bridge across the Merderet River. However, as German pressure increased against the beleagured American defenders of Chef du Pont during the ensuing hours of combat, serious consideration was given to blowing the bridge to stall a German counterattack against the paratroopers on the east side of the Merderet. This bridgehead, which would be strategically important for the advance of the 90th Infantry coming over the beaches, was held, however, to a large extent due to the efforts of LTC Thomas Shanley's tenacious defense of a key blocking position on the west side of the Merderet which kept the Germans from massing for a decisive counterattack against Chef du Pont.

La Fière continued to prove a tough nut for the 505th and the additional paratroopers sent by Gavin. While supervising the assaults of la Fière and Chef du Pont, Gavin met Maj Gen Ridgway who had jumped in with the paratroopers. Ridgway ordered that the la Fière causeway and bridge must be taken at all costs and the area cleared of Germans. As a result, Col Roy Lindquist of the 508th Parachute Infantry took charge of the assorted paratroopers and struck at the bridge once again. One company under Capt Ben Schwartzwalder (later to win fame as the football coach at Syracuse) drove its way across the bridge; however, Schwartzwalder's men then continued to drive on rather than staying to garrison the far side of the bridge. Spearheaded by tanks, the Germans moved into the vacuum to retake the bridge, though they did lose three tanks to rocket fire and gammon grenades delivered by a small blocking force under Lt Louis Levy of the 507th Parachute Infantry. Unfortunately, the chance to hold the west side of the la Fière bridgehead was thus lost as the Germans held it for two more days. The 82nd, however, continued to interdict the east side of the la Fière causeway thus preventing the Germans from advancing as well. Fortunately, one 57mm anti-tank gun had been retrieved from a glider and set up on the eastern side of the bridge. It knocked out an advancing Renault tank which helped block the bridge thus slowing any German counterattack. So heavy did the firing become on the part of the paratroopers battling for the eastern la Fière causeway, that their machine guns would 'cook-off' some fifteen to twenty rounds when the triggers were released due to the heat of the chamber.

Capt Schwartzwalder, who had managed to drive across the la Fière bridge, was from the 507th Parachute Infantry, which was badly scattered during the drop. Only two sticks from the 507th actually landed within the regimental DZ, while some were scattered as much as 20 miles (32km) away. Many descended in the Merderet River. So badly scattered was the 507th, in fact, that there was little possibility of operating cohesively as a regiment. Instead, the paratroopers operated in small groups or joined with other regiments.

The 508th Parachute Infantry managed to get seven sticks into the regimental DZ but otherwise fared little better than the 507th. Quite a few members of the 508th, in fact, landed within the 101st Airborne area and fought alongside the Screaming Eagles (later, no doubt, claiming to have been the reason for the 101st's successes!) One small group of 508th paratroopers under Lt Malcomb Brennan did manage to add materially to

Depressed and tired 82nd Airborne trooper captured after jumping into occupied France during Operation Overlord. (*Bundesarchiv*)

German confusion within the 82nd area by killing Gen Wilhelm Falley, the commanding general of the German 91st Infantry Division when they ambushed his car.

Another member of the 508th, LTC Thomas J. B. Shanley, the CO of the 2/508th, assembled a miscellaneous group of paratroopers and headed for his battalion's objective, a bridge over the Douve River. Meeting stiff resistance, however, Shanley and his men withdrew to Hill 30 where they held off German counterattacks for two days, thus holding what came to be considered the key position in the entire 82nd Division area since they interdicted the German route of advance to Chef du Pont and then on to Ste Mère-Eglise.

Although gliders carrying 57mm anti-tank guns had landed shortly after the paratroopers, the major glider landings were scheduled for the evening of D-Day. However, LZ W where the gliders were scheduled to land was still hotly contested. Unfortunately, due to his long range communication equipment having been dropped in the Merderet River, Ridgway was not able to warn the gliders off. Realizing the glider assault was eminent, an attempt was made to force the Germans from their positions around the LZ W by 82nd Airborne paratroopers, advance elements of the 4th US

Infantry Division and Edson Raff's force of tanks and glider men driving inland from the beachhead. Some of Raff's tanks, however, were knocked out by German 88mm guns and the Germans held their positions. No cancel orders having been received from Ridgway, the gliders were actually sent in an hour early, arriving over LZ W at about 20.00 hours. Many landed off course, which proved fortuitous as they avoided the heaviest concentration of German fire. Natural and man-made obstacles proved to be the greatest danger to the gliders in any case, taking an extremely heavy toll. It soon became obvious that the smaller CG4As had proven more survivable than the much larger Horsas.

The next morning, beginning a little after 07.00 hours, the remaining glidermen of the 325th Glider Infantry began landing. Though they had the advantage of coming in during daylight, they still had problems with the broken Normandy landscape, suffering thirty-five killed and 137 injured during the landings.

Having gathered together as many glidermen as he could, on D+1 Raff fought his way to Ridgway. A few days later, Raff was given command of the 507th Parachute Infantry Regiment because Col Millett, the regimental commander, had been captured after landing.

One battalion of the 325th was immediately sent to help the paratroopers fighting to take the la Fière bridge, for, though by the morning of 8 June the 82nd was in control of most of its objectives and was mopping up throughout the airhead, the la Fière bridge remained in German hands. Late on 8 June, however, Ridgway learned that there was a submerged road across the Merderet. At 23.00 hours, he ordered the 1/325th to infiltrate across the river and hit the Germans holding the la Fière bridge on their flank.

During this operation, one platoon of the 1/325th was cut off. The Germans, sensing easy prey, were moving in for the kill when one gliderman, PFC Charles N. DeGlopper, leaped up and gave covering fire with his BAR while the remainder of his platoon slipped away to safety. Killed in the course of his heroic act, DeGlopper received a posthumous Congressional Medal of Honor, the only one awarded to a member of the 82nd Airborne at Normandy. Despite DeGlopper's heroism and his battalion's attempt to flank the Germans, the la Fière bridge was held until another assault was launched, this time spearheaded by the 3/325th and a parachute company and backed by artillery and tank support. With great difficulty, this assault finally cleared the bridge on the morning of 9 June, thus taking what had proven to be the toughest 82nd objective.

Once the bridge was taken, Brig Gen Gavin then led a drive to link up with LTC Shanley who was still holding out on Hill 30 despite heavy pressure from the Germans. Sporadic artillery support from 75mm howitzers of the 319th Field Artillery at Chef du Pont had helped Shanley's men during their long wait for reinforcements. As it turned out, however, la Fière was still not completely secured as one more aggressive German counterattack still had to be fought off.

Despite the badly scattered drops, the All Americans had fought almost continuously for three days. On D-Day alone, the division had suffered 1,259 casualties, and this number continued to mount. It is very likely, though, that the airborne casualties prevented even higher losses on the part of the assault troops coming across Utah Beach since the paratroopers were blocking many of the German units which could have hit the amphibious forces while they were coming ashore.

Once the beachhead was secure, the 82nd Airborne was used as assault infantry, driving on to the west to help to cut off the Cotentin Peninsula. The 82nd's final major assault of the Normandy Campaign came when all four All American infantry regiments drove across the Douve and the Prairies Marecageuses for miles then southeast to seize the high ground over La Haye-du-Puits. By the time they were finally pulled back to England during the second week in July, the All Americans had seen thirty-three days of continuous combat, suffering 5,245 casualties in the process. An indication of the fact that airborne officers led from the front is that fifteen regimental or battalion commanders were among the casualties.

Although the men of the 82nd Airborne were glad to return to England, where they found many of their buddies whose fate had remained unknown during the chaos of the drop and combat in Normandy, the All Americans also realized that there were many friends they would never see again. Passes to see the English girlfriends many paratroopers had acquired while training in England prior to the drop helped to salve the physical and emotional wounds, however, and soon training began for a new operation, focussing the men of the 82nd on their next objective. Now battle-hardened by combat in Sicily, Italy and Normandy, the All Americans were among the most proven US divisions. It was a distinction which was not likely to leave the 82nd idle for long.

6 AIRBORNE CARPET TO THE RHINE

As the Allied armies, spearheaded by Patton's Third Army, broke out across France during the summer of 1944, overrunning entire German armies, hopes grew for a rapid coup de grâce to the Reich. Since the advance had been more rapid than many had envisaged, Eisenhower found himself faced with choosing where his primary thrust would now be delivered and, more to the point, whether Montgomery or Bradley would lead it. Montgomery advocated a drive through Belgium and into the Ruhr, thus severing Hitler's industrial sinews, while Bradley lobbied for a drive across the Rhine south of Frankfurt.

Eisenhower, as Supreme Commander, had to weigh the advantages of both plans. Montgomery's plan appealed to him because it would allow the rapid capture of the vital port of Antwerp and the overrunning of the German V2 sites which were raining a deadly hail of rockets on London and south-east England. On the other hand, Montgomery's reputation for slow and methodical advances left Eisenhower in some doubt as to how rapidly Montgomery's 21st Army Group would move if given priority. Bradley's 12th Army Group, on the other hand, was 100 miles (160km) in front of Montgomery and was spearheaded by George Patton, about whose aggressiveness Eisenhower had little doubt.

Eisenhower's decision was to compromise, giving priority to Montgomery's 21st Army Group until he reached Antwerp, and then Bradley's 12th Army Group would receive priority for the push across the Rhine. Montgomery advanced rapidly, liberating Brussels on 3 September and Antwerp the next day, though unfortunately the 54-mile (87km) estuary leading to the sea remained in German hands, thus negating much of the port's usefulness. Still, Montgomery drove on, pushing into Holland on 12 September.

While the strategy for the drive on Berlin had been under debate, the 82nd Airborne Division had become part of the 1st Allied Airborne Army which had been activated on 2 August 1944, under the command of Air Force Lt Gen Lewis Brereton, (who had been involved in Billy Mitchell's World War One airborne plans). The 1st Allied Airborne Army included the US XVIIIth Airborne Corps, commanded by Matthew Ridgway and consisting of the US 17th, 82nd and 101st Airborne Divisions, British airborne forces and certain troop carrier assets. Brereton's deputy was Gen 'Boy' Browning, the British airborne general.

Due to Ridgway's promotion, Brig Gen Gavin had taken command of the 82nd on 16 August, though he had yet to receive his second star. Since Ridgway had taken much of his divisional staff along with him, Gavin's first priority was the selection of a new staff for the 82nd. Gavin's selections had a chance to learn their job rapidly, too, because Brereton's staff prepared eighteen different plans for the use of airborne forces ahead of the Allied advance. Though the 82nd was not included in all of the plans, preparations were continually underway for an impending operation which would then be canceled because ground troops had overrun the objective before the airborne operation could be mounted. Two noteworthy objectives the 82nd was alerted to expect as assignations were Tournai and Liege, both in Belgium. Both operations were, however, called off.

On 5 September, the 1st Allied Airborne Army was offered to Montgomery to help speed his drive through the Low Countries. Montgomery accepted the offer with alacrity, offering a plan which was one of the most daring of the war and which astounded those who thought of him as overly cautious. Codenamed Operation MARKET GARDEN, this plan called for the use of three airborne divisions plus a brigade to lay an 'airborne carpet' from Eindhoven to Arnhem, with the paratroopers and glidermen seizing and holding five key bridges along the route while armored forces pushed forward rapidly to relieve the paratroopers and then thrust on across the Rhine at Arnhem, thus flanking the Siegfried Line. The airborne phase of the plan would be codenamed MARKET, while the ground phase, which called for the British XXX Corps under Gen Horrocks to drive forward along the airborne carpet through Arnhem deep into Holland, would be codenamed GARDEN.

The three primary objectives of the operation were to cut off German forces in Holland, to outflank the Siegfried Line and to cross the Rhine at Arnhem. During the initial discussions, Browning, representing the 1st Allied Airborne Army, appreciated the boldness of Montgomery's plan but had reservations about the ability of the armored spearhead to link up with the airborne forces in time. It was during these discussions that Browning uttered the famous comment about the bridge at Arnhem: 'We may be going a bridge too far.'

Despite Browning's reservations, the plan was approved on 10 September with the airborne phase scheduled to be launched one week later on 17 September. Immediately, the 1st Allied Airborne Army sprang into action, preparing almost thirty-five thousand airborne troops for combat. Since their return to England in July, the men of the 82nd had trained new recruits to bring the units decimated during the Italian and Normandy operations back to strength and had prepared themselves mentally and physically for their next operation. When Gavin received orders to report for a briefing on the afternoon of 10 September, that operation was only a week away.

At the initial Operation MARKET briefing, objectives were assigned partially by locations of the divisions in the United Kingdom and partially because the British 1st Airborne had earlier planned an operation in the Arnhem area which had been one of those aborted. Unlike previous operations, it was decided this would be carried out in daylight because the Allies could maintain air superiority and the daylight drop would prevent many of the problems with scattering encountered on previous operations. As the objectives were broken down, the British 1st Airborne Division and the Polish 1st Parachute Brigade were assigned Arnhem; the 101st Airborne Division was assigned the southern bridges closest to the start point for XXX Corps; and the All Americans were assigned a 10-mile strip between Nijmegen and Grave, including bridges over the Maas and Waal.

Initially, it was foreseen that 2,500 gliders would be used in addition to all of the parachute troops. To escort the massive airborne armada would be 1,500 fighters. However, the problem soon encountered by Gen Browning, who had been given command of the airborne forces involved, was that there were just not enough transport aircraft available to lift all of the parachutists and pull all of the gliders at once. As a result, it was reluctantly decided to send in the airborne forces incrementally.

Since the 82nd would have to hold longer than the 101st because it was further along the 'carpet' and would have to seize and hold the critical Groesbeek Ridge, it was a necessity that the All Americans have their artillery as rapidly as possible. Therefore, in addition to parachute artillery which would be dropped with the infantry regiments, fifty gliders carrying jeeps and anti-tank guns would land with the initial wave of All Americans. A further 450 gliders would come in on D+1 carrying the 325th Glider Infantry and additional artillery.

The division staffs had to choose their DZs and LZs quickly. The 82nd's choices were made on the basis of four priorities: first, the Groesbeek Heights; second, the Grave bridge, third, the Maas-Waal Canal crossings; and fourth, the Waal bridge at Nijmegen. The 504th Parachute Infantry was back at full strength and so rejoined their comrades in the 82nd, while the 507th, which had jumped with the All Americans in Normandy, left divisional control prior to the jump in Holland. Therefore, the DZs were assigned as follows: the 505th Parachute Infantry and the 376th Parachute Field Artillery would jump into DZ N, which was located between the Groesbeek Heights and the Reichswald; the 508th Parachute Infantry would jump into DZ T, which was just to the north of DZ N; the 504th Parachute Infantry would jump into a DZ which was on the west side of the Groesbeek Heights between the Maas River and the Maas-Waal Canal. One 504th company would jump separately near the western end of the Grave bridge so that it could be rapidly assaulted from both ends.

The 505th Parachute Infantry would have the mission of securing the town of Groesbeek and setting up a defensive line along the base of the Groesbeek Heights, while the 376th Parachute Field Artillery positioned its 75mm guns to fire upon any German force attempting to advance out of the Reichswald. The 508th Parachute Infantry's missions would be to secure DZ T so that the main glider landings could come in on D+1, to occupy the Groesbeek Heights between Wyler and Nijmegen, to help the 504th capture Maas-Waal Canal bridges, and to take the large Waal River bridge at Nijmegen. The 504th Parachute Infantry had as its primary

During July 1944, ordnance specialists of the 82nd Airborne inventory weapons. Note that the two men on the right wear the para-glider badge on their sidecaps indicating qualification in both. (*US Army*)

mission the capture of the Maas River bridge at Grave and along with the 508th to seize the Maas-Waal Canal bridges, at least one of which had to be taken intact and held. The 505th's DZ was the one into which Gen Browning would come via glider on D-Day.

On 14 September, the divisional commanders met with Browning to discuss their plans for carrying out their divisional missions. Gavin and Browning both agreed that before the Nijmegen bridge was assaulted, it was necessary that all of the other 82nd objectives must be secured, yet the Nijmegen bridge remained a critical objective. Hitting hard and fast would be an absolute necessity for the paratroopers, but that's what the All Americans did best!

Initial intelligence reports showed that no powerful German units would be available to oppose the drops, but additional information forty-eight hours before the drop showed German armor in the area. In fact, two

'Slim Jim' Gavin briefs his officers prior to the 82nd's jump into Holland as part of Market Garden. (*US Army*)

SS Panzer divisions, which were admittedly depleted after the fighting in France but still a formidable foe for lightly armed airborne forces, were identified in the Arnhem area. As a result, consideration was given to dropping a second airborne division at Arnhem, but the plan remained essentially the same.

By 15 September, the troopers of the 82nd had been cloistered behind barbed wire prior to the jump and were drawing ammunition and equipment. While drawing their equipment, the men of the 82nd created a minor run on anti-tank mines as those jumping on D-Day would take in two thousand of the Panzer-killers with them. While waiting to emplane, the members of the 504th made repeated references to the fact they would be jumping into their 'Grave' but this was just typical of the gallows humor of the same paratroopers who loved singing such favorites as 'Blood on the Risers', reproduced here.

Blood on the Risers
To the tune of 'Battle Hymn of the Republic'

'Is everyone happy? cried the sergeant looking up,
Our Hero feebly answered 'Yes,' and then they stood him up,
He leaped right out into the blast, his static line unhooked,
    He ain't gonna jump no more!
        CHORUS
        Gory, Gory, what a helluva way to die!
        Gory, Gory, what a helluva way to die!
        Gory, Gory, what a helluva way to die!
          He ain't gonna jump no more!

He counted long; he counted loud; he waited for the shock;
He felt the wind; he felt the clouds; he felt the awful drop;
He jerked the cord; the silk spilled out and wrapped around his legs.
    He ain't gonna jump no more!
        CHORUS

The risers wrapped around his neck; connectors cracked his dome;
The lines were snarled and tied in knots, around his skinny bones;
The canopy became his shroud as he hurtled to the ground.
    He ain't gonna jump no more!
        CHORUS

The days he's lived and loved and laughed kept running through his mind;
He thought about the girl back home, the one he left behind;
He thought about the medics and wondered what they'd find.
    He ain't gonna jump no more!
        CHORUS

The ambulance was on the spot; the jeeps were running wild;
The medics jumped and screamed with glee; they rolled their sleeves and smiled,
For it had been a week or so since a chute had failed.
    He ain't gonna jump no more!
        CHORUS

He hit the ground, the sound was 'Splatt,' his blood went spurting high;
His comrades then were heard to say, 'A helluva way to die.'
He lay there rolling round the welter of his gore.
    He ain't gonna jump no more!
        CHORUS

There was blood upon the risers; there were brains upon the 'chute;
Intestines were a'dangling from his paratrooper's boots;
They picked him up still in his 'chute and poured him from his boots.
    He ain't gonna jump no more!
        CHORUS

Whether singing 'Blood on the Risers' or joking about the jump over Grave, however, the men of the 82nd Airborne were just mentally preparing themselves to leap into the tempest of battle once again. To make MARKET as safe as possible for the airborne forces who would be going in on 17 September, more than one thousand bomber sorties were flown against German airfields and anti-aircraft installations during the twenty-four hours preceding the take off of the 1,545 transports and 478 gliders which would carry the airborne assault force to Holland.

When the first of the 480 transports carrying the All Americans to Holland took off at 11.09 hours, the recent replacements heading for their first combat jump felt the normal mixture of fear and exhilaration that men going into combat for the first time feel, while the veterans of the jumps in Sicily, Salerno and Normandy wondered what their first daylight combat jump would hold. Maj Gen Ridgway, now commanding the XVIIIth Airborne Corps, still managed to accompany the 82nd to battle as he flew along in a B-17 to observe the drop.

A few of the C-47s carrying the 82nd took hits, but the flak was not as heavy as on previous missions. Most of the planes which were damaged even managed to deliver their sticks over the drop zones. The 82nd's pathfinders jumped at 12.47 hours followed by the first sticks of the 505th Parachute Infantry at 13.00. In all, 7,277 All Americans jumped over Holland while 209 more arrived by glider. As almost all of the paratroopers drifted down right on their DZs, it became obvious that this was the most accurate drop of the war so far.

Despite the massive bombardment which had preceded the airborne drops, the Germans were taken completely by surprise. As was his practice, Brig Gen Gavin was in the lead plane and so was one of the first members of the division to touch down in Holland. Shortly after landing, a Dutch officer accompanying Gavin began using the telephone in a nearby house to contact members of the Dutch resistance to get information about the Germans' disposition and about the airborne landings in the 101st and British 1st areas.

As the paratroopers drifted towards their DZs, those coming down near anti-aircraft guns actually steered their parachutes towards the guns, frequently using their .45 pistols to take the gunners under fire as they descended. Private Edwin Robb, for example, unlimbered his SMG upon landing and with his bullet-riddled chute dragging behind him, single-handedly attacked one gun crew, killing one, capturing the others and then destroying the gun with plastic explosive.

As a direct result of the accurate drop, Rueben Tucker's 504th Parachute Infantry managed to seize both ends of the Maas River bridge at Grave, quickly taking advantage of surprise and the fact that the 22mm anti-aircraft guns in the flak towers on the bridge could not depress far enough to engage the paratroopers landing so near the bridge. Once again thanks to the accurate drop, Col

William Ekman's 505th Parachute Infantry managed to take the town of Groesbeek rapidly.

Though the Nijmegen bridge was of utmost importance for allowing an eventual linkup between XXX Corps and the British airborne forces striking at Arnhem, Gavin and Browning had agreed that all other 82nd objectives had to take priority over it. Still, late on D-Day, the commander of the 1/508th, LTC Shields Warren Jr, led two of his companies into Nijmegen where they did manage to disable the controls for the explosives on the bridge, which they located in the post office. However, the men of the 508th met stiff resistance and were not able to seize the bridge from the tenacious defenders from the 10th SS Panzer Division.

Another failure occurred when members of the 505th and 504th could not prevent the Germans from blowing the canal bridges at Hatert and Malden, though fortunately the bridge at Molenhoek was seized intact thus giving XXX Corps one bridge to carry on their advance. The fourth of the canal bridges at Honinghutie was also severely damaged thus making it absolutely necessary that the one intact bridge be held at all costs.

As D-Day ended, it was becoming clear that there were problems throughout the area of operations. XXX Corps' advance had been stalled short of Eindhoven, which was just as well since the 101st Airborne had yet to seize the town. The 82nd had not yet secured the Nijmegen bridge nor had the 1st Airborne yet taken Arnhem bridge. The British airborne forces were, in fact, meeting ever stiffening resistance.

Contributing greatly to the successes of the 82nd was the 376th Parachute Field Artillery which was making the first large scale combat parachute artillery insertion of the war. Within an hour of jumping, the gunners of the 376th had ten howitzers in action and during the first twenty-four hours of combat fired 315 rounds to help to keep the Germans from mounting a counterattack. In addition, members of the 376th had managed to capture over four hundred German prisoners.

During the night of D-Day and the early hours of D+1, one patrol of the 82nd stopped a train full of Germans by hitting the engine with a bazooka rocket. Throughout the 82nd area during the night, the paratroopers dug in to hold their gains until XXX Corps' arrival, though some members of Col Roy Lindquist's 508th had their hands full as they found themselves digging in on German soil just across the border, thus facing heavy counterattacks from Germans anxious to protect the Fatherland for symbolic reasons. To make things even tougher for those members of the 508th defending the Groesbeek Ridge, the fight for the Nijmegen bridge was denuding the defenses, thus allowing the Germans to occupy the glider LZs where 450 gliders would be coming in the next afternoon. Realizing that his lines were rapidly being eroded, Gavin ordered the 3/508th to break off fighting for Nijmegen on the morning of 18 September and re-secure the area around the LZs. Throughout the 82nd area, in fact, the paratroopers found themselves beating off German counterattacks.

As the afternoon glider landings approached, the 3/508th and two companies of the 307th Airborne Engineer Battalion fought tenaciously to secure the LZs, managing to clear most of the area by the time the gliders began to arrive. Just before 14.00 hours, the first gliders appeared overhead and began swooping towards the barely secured landing zones. Within thirty minutes, the last glider was down, having delivered the 319th and 320th Glider Field Artillery, the 456th Parachute Field Artillery, the remainder of the 307th Airborne Engineers, the 80th Airborne Anti-aircraft Artillery and a company of airborne medical personnel. To augment the equipment which had been dropped on D-Day, thirty howitzers, eight 57mm anti-tank guns and over ninety jeeps had come in on gliders. The landing had gone extremely well with the exception of twenty-five gliders of the 319th Glider Field Artillery which had overshot the LZ and landed about five miles inside Germany, though eventually about half of the troops aboard these gliders made it back to rejoin the division.

Shortly after the glider landing, a parachute re-supply mission came in, with the All Americans successfully recovering about eighty per cent of the food, ammunition and other *matériel* which was dropped. This, it should be noted, is a quite acceptable percentage of recovery on a combat re-supply mission. It should also be noted that in anticipation of losses, airborne re-supply bundles were normally packed with substantial redundancy.

The reinforcements aboard the gliders were greatly appreciated, especially the enhanced firepower of the artillery pieces, as the 82nd found itself battling for control of its area against stiffening German counterattacks. The All Americans knew now, however, if they could hold a while longer they would link up with XXX Corps as the Guards Armoured Division had punched through to link up with the 101st Airborne at Eindhoven and was driving on to link up with the All Americans at the Grave bridge. This linkup was successfully made on the morning of 19 September when both Gen Browning, who had come into the 82nd area on the first day aboard a glider, and Gen Gavin met the Guards Armoured spearhead.

The arrival of the British tanks allowed Gavin a little more tactical leeway and thus he took the 2/505th which had been acting as his reserve, and committed them against the Nijmegen bridge. Meanwhile, fighting remained heavy in the 508th Parachute Infantry area as the Germans kept probing to break through the 82nd's rather thinly held perimeter.

By late on 19 September, though virtually no communication had come through from Arnhem other than reports through the Dutch underground, Gavin, with the instincts of an experienced airborne commander, knew that the 1st Airborne badly needed reinforcement. However, the Nijmegen bridge was still not secure as the German defenders continued to mount a tenacious defense. Browning was also growing concerned about the fate of the 1st Airborne and ordered Gavin to take the bridge as rapidly as possible.

As a result, Gavin asked Gen Horrocks for the use of any boats carried by XXX Corps' combat engineers so that the 504th Parachute Infantry could make an assault crossing of the Waal. Horrocks concurred and ordered the canvas assault boats to be brought forward as soon as possible. Gavin's plan was to cross at the point where the Waal Canal entered the lower Waal River, hitting the German positions on the opposite bank with all the artillery and tank fire he could muster, including smoke rounds to cover the crossing. Initially, he planned for the 504th to set off at 08.00 hours on 20 September, but the boats had not arrived by that time so the crossing had to be postponed.

Meanwhile, fighting rooftop to rooftop with the support of the Grenadier Guards, the 2/505th pushed the German force on the southern end of the Nijmegen railway and highway bridges back, but did not dislodge them.

On the afternoon of 20 September, while still waiting for the assault boats, Gavin received word that the Germans were putting heavy pressure on his eastern flank at Mook and Beek, thus threatening the absolutely critical Molenhoek Canal bridge. Leaving the crossing of the Waal in the competent hands of Rueben Tucker, Gavin rushed to take personal command of his threatened flank. Against their opposite numbers of the German 6th Fallschirmjäger Division, the 505th Parachute Infantry managed to retake Mook after bloody building-to-building fighting.

Mook re-secured, Gavin then rejoined the 508th which was dug in near

82nd Airborne troopers emplaning for the jump into Holland. (*US Army*)

Beek and told them that if they could hold until the next day, he hoped the 325th Glider Infantry, whose arrival had been delayed by bad weather over the take-off airfields, would be arriving to reinforce them. Paratroopers, though they can defend tenaciously if necessary, are better on the offense so the 508th did not just hold, they went on the attack, retaking Beek on the night of 20/21 September. In fact, they drove the Germans all the way back to the Rhine.

While the eastern flank was being secured, the 3/504th had finally begun crossing the Waal a little before 15.00 hours on 20 September. Despite the smoke screen and the covering fire, the boats took heavy German fire, some sinking or being blown up. Nevertheless, the paratroopers pushed on, going in with bayonets and grenades as soon as their boats touched the opposite bank. The paratroopers, in fact, attacked with especial ferocity after having to endure the tormenting fire from the shore during the crossing. The boats which survived the crossing turned around to bring in another load of paratroopers. Some idea of the difficulty of an assault crossing of the Waal at this point can be gained from the fact that the German commanders not on the scene would not at first believe the Americans were attempting an opposed crossing.

Not only were the Americans attempting a crossing, however, they were succeeding. Under Captains Thomas M. Burriss and Carl W. Koppel, the paratroopers headed for the bridges and by 17.00 hours, had gained control of the northern end. Simultaneously, the 2/505th and Grenadier Guards hit the southern end of the Nijmegen bridge once again, breaking through at about 18.00 hours. During the crossing and battle for the bridge, the 504th alone had suffered about two hundred killed, but what many considered the most critical objective on the road to Arnhem had finally been secured.

Though there was still some fear the Nijmegen bridge would be blown up by the Germans, the first Grenadier Guards tank started across the bridge just before 19.00 hours. Once across, the tankers joined the paratroopers to dig in and hold the bridge. It was just as well they did, too, for at about noon on 21 September the All Americans had to fight off a counterattack against the bridge, during which Private John R. Towle single-handedly drove off two German tanks with his bazooka and destroyed a house containing nine Germans, thus breaking the back of the counterattack. Unfortunately, Towle died in the process, though he won a posthumous Congressional Medal of Honor for his heroism.

Despite the heroic actions of the 82nd in taking the Nijmegen bridge, the 1st Airborne was in deep trouble at Arnhem. So precarious was their situation, in fact, that XXX Corps halted their advance temporarily until the situation stabilised. By 21 September, the 1st Airborne was already being compressed into a small pocket around Oosterbeek. Eventually, only about two thousand of the 9,500 men who landed at Arnhem would manage to filter back across the river. Arnhem had, indeed, proved to be a 'bridge too far.' Despite the heroic actions of the 82nd and 101st Airborne Divisions, the stand of the 1st Airborne has obscured many of the accomplishments of the American paratroopers during MARKET GARDEN. Just during MARKET GARDEN, for example, the 82nd had suffered 1,432 casualties and would suffer even more as 'leg' infantry before being pulled back.

Even without the Arnhem bridge, the Nijmegen bridge remained an important objective. As a result, the *Luftwaffe* launched attack after attack with their new jet aircraft and German combat swimmers attacked the bridge, but both were unsuccessful. With troops from XXX Corps holding the bridge, the 504th was pulled back to help to stabilise the 82nd's defensive lines. Reinforced by the 325th Glider Infantry on 23 September, the division took up positions from Reithorst to the Maas River.

Not long after they had assumed these new positions, the British general, Sir Miles Dempsey, visited the 82nd area and commented to Gavin, 'I'm proud to meet the Commanding General of the finest division in the world today.'

One noteworthy battle prize captured by the 504th Parachute Infantry about this time was a truck load of Panzerfausts, an anti-armor weapon which they much preferred to the bazooka and which they continued to use against German tanks for the rest of the war.

On 8 October, the 82nd was transferred to XXX Corps control, a move that might have met with more griping had not Horrocks been very popular with the tough paratroopers. While under XXX Corps control some 82nd officers got a chance to meet King George VI, whom they thought a very kind man. October also saw Gavin finally get his second star as he was promoted to the rank of major general.

On 13 November 1944, the 82nd was pulled back to Rheims, France, for rest and replacements, though Gavin immediately had ammunition issued in case the division was needed as a 'fire brigade.' Since the German Ardennes Offensive was not far off, this move proved almost prophetic on Gavin's part. The 101st Airborne was also stationed at Rheims so the All Americans and Screaming Eagles got a chance to stay in fighting trim by battling with each other in the local bars.

7 THE BULGE

The interlude the 82nd spent in billets at Suippes and Sissone after being pulled out of Holland was rather pleasant—if brawling with members of the 101st, working in replacements recently graduated from the locally established jump school and explaining to French girls in creative ways why paratroopers bloused their trousers can be called pleasant! The All American rumor mill was at work during the fall of 1944 and, though the paratroopers were disappointed that their efforts in Holland had not brought the early end to the war they had hoped for, they happily discussed the 'poop' that they were going to jump over Berlin and end the war with a lightning airborne assault. This rumor came close to becoming fact late in the war as serious consideration was given to launching an airborne assault on the heart of the Reich.

Then, at 05.30 hours on 16 December 1944, the Germans launched their surprise offensive through the Ardennes, catching the Americans completely by surprise. The 82nd and 101st were, at the time, about the

A T-24 light tank of the 740th Tank Battalion assigned to the 82nd Airborne Division at Nonceveux, Belgium early in 1945. (*US Army*)

82nd Airborne pack howitzer in action against the Germans during the Battle of the Bulge. (*US Army*)

only reserves SHAEF had at its disposal; therefore, as the news began to come through on 17 December of the seriousness of the German penetration, Maj Gen Gavin followed developments carefully. Gavin's interest in the progress of the battle became even more marked when he realized that he was the acting commander of the XVIIIth Airborne Corps since Ridgway was in England at the time and Maxwell Taylor, the CO of the 101st Airborne, has been sent to the USA as Ridgway's representative at discussions about reorganizing the airborne divisions. While having dinner with his staff on 17 December, Gavin was alerted that the XVIIIth Airborne Corps had to be ready to move within twenty-four hours if needed, and it looked as if they were needed!

Since the 82nd had had the most rest, having been pulled out of Holland before the 101st, and since Gavin had already had ammunition and food for four days issued to his regiments, Gavin ordered the All Americans to move out at daylight on 18 December, with the 101st following a few hours later. Just before midnight, Gavin himself left for the headquarters in Belgium of 1st Army commander Courtney Hodges, under whom he would be serving, arriving at about 09.00 hours on the morning of 18 December. During the discussions with Hodges, it was decided that since the 82nd was already on the move, the All Americans would bypass Bastogne to occupy the high ground around Werbomont to help to turn the German thrust southward, while the 101st following behind would occupy the critical blocking point at Bastogne. This decision thus assured the Screaming Eagles their 'rendezvous with destiny' at Bastogne.

When Gavin arrived at Werbomont, he was told by engineer units in the area that they were preparing to blow the bridges on the line of the German advance. Gavin then proceeded to Bastogne where he told Brig Gen McAuliffe, the acting CO of the 101st Airborne, to hold it until receiving orders to the contrary. By the time Gavin returned to Werbomont to take command of his division, the paratroopers were arriving and immediately moving into defensive positions.

By 19 December, Ridgway had arrived in Belgium and taken command of his corps from Werbomont, thus freeing Gavin to concentrate on command of the All Americans. As Gavin inspected his positions on the morning of 19 December, he discovered that the road linking Werbomont to Bastogne had been cut. Gavin also had received orders from Ridgway to deploy his troops well outside of Werbomont to secure the largest possible area. As a result, troops of the 325th Glider Infantry were deployed to Barvaux

Troops of the 740th Tank Battalion, attached to the 82nd Airborne during the Battle of the Bulge. (*US Army*)

Late in December 1944, Maj Gen Gavin walking down a lane in the Erria Area where the 3rd Battalion, 508th Parachute Infantry had wiped out a battalion of attacking SS troopers while holding during the Battle of the Bulge. Note that in keeping with his policy of leading from the front, Gavin is armed with an M1 Garand rifle as well as his .45 pistol. (*US Army*)

to the west and Grandmenil and Mouhan to the south. Paratroopers of the 505th Parachute Infantry were sent to Habiemont on 19 December and then on the Basse-Bodeux and Trois Ponts to the east the following day. The 504th Parachute Infantry was sent to Rahier and then further east to Cheneux and Trois Ponts over the next couple of days. Finally, the 508th Parachute Infantry moved southeast to Vielsalm and took up positions on the dominating heights of Their Dumont. As the division's artillery arrived, Gavin ordered the gunners into positions where they could support the paratroopers who were soon likely to be in conflict with German tanks.

As was frequently the case, Rueben Tucker's 504th Parachute Infantry were among the first All Americans to go into combat. On the afternoon of 20 December, as they attacked a battalion of the 2nd SS Panzer Grenadier Regiment, Tucker's battle-hardened paratroopers got a chance to put the Panzerfausts they had captured in Holland to good use against German halftracks and flakwagons at Cheneux. After hand-to-hand combat during which they inflicted their first German losses during the Battle of the Bulge, the Devils in Baggy Pants captured fourteen Flakwagons and a battery of 105mm howitzers, but at the cost of 225 American casualties. Proud of their newly acquired German equipment, the 504th jokingly referred to themselves as the '504th Parachute Armored Regiment.' However, their humor would not have lasted had they realized the battalion which they had fought had been involved in the infamous Malmedy massacre of American prisoners. Had they possessed this knowledge at the time, it is doubtful that even the thirty-four prisoners taken by the 504th at Cheneux would have been allowed to surrender.

While the 504th was gaining their victory, at St Vith to the east and Bastogne to the south the Germans had surrounded and cut off the American defenders, thus it became even more critical for the 82nd to hold its positions. Therefore, the 2/505th defending Trois Ponts set up positions along the Salm River with the intent of denying the Germans a crossing. About daylight on 21 December, elements of the 1st SS Panzer Division launched an attack against the battalion's positions. Due to the tenacity of the paratroopers—battle-proven in Sicily, Italy, Normandy and Holland—and the rough terrain which favored the defense, LTC Ben Vandervoort's 2/505th was holding back one of the best divisions in the German Army. Due to the critical nature of the positions Vandervoort was holding, Gavin offered to reinforce him, though it would be at the expense of another portion of the 82nd's defenses. Vandervoort, however, confident in his men, told Gavin they would hold without reinforcements. Gavin knew his subordinates and if Vandervoort said he would hold, Gavin was confident he would; the 2/505th was not reinforced.

While the 504th and 505th were in action, things were relatively quiet for the 508th Parachute Infantry on Their Dumont heights and to their right where the 325th Glider Infantry, short of one battalion in division-al reserve, was anchoring the right side of the 82nd's somewhat elastic defensive positions, which by the morning of 21 December extended from Cheneux to Hebronval.

The right of the 82nd's defenses was not spared the attentions of the Germans for long; on the afternoon of 22 December, a German armored force drove against the 325th, forcing them to withdraw, though the 82nd's 75mm howitzers inflicted heavy losses on the Germans. The German near breakthrough was soon halted when engineers blew a bridge and the reserve battalion of the 325th was committed to the battle just in time to hold the Germans in check. One bonus which accrued to the All Americans during the 325th's struggle was the capture of German documents showing their intention of turning the 82nd's right flank and advancing through Werbomont. It looked as if the small town of Fraiture and the area around it would prove a critical blocking position and would receive the brunt of the German attack.

In an attempt to reinforce his right flank, Gavin rushed a battalion of the 504th Parachute Infantry to bolster the defenses, thus extending the 82nd's front to about 25 miles. Meanwhile, to the south at Bastogne, on 22

In April, 1945, men of the 82nd Airborne Division prepare to board a train en route for northern Germany. (*US Army*)

December Brig Gen McAuliffe had given the Germans his famous reply, 'Nuts!', upon being asked to surrender and the 101st was holding despite heavy German pressure. Having battled alongside the Screaming Eagles in Normandy and Holland and against them in bars all over France and England, the All Americans realised the Germans had their work cut out for them at Bastogne. More to the point, though, the men of the 82nd wanted to make sure the Germans had just as much difficulty with them.

The Germans continued to increase their pressure against the 82nd as the 9th SS Panzer Division launched an attack against the 508th Parachute Infantry, which was holding open a corridor for the units retreating after an heroic stand at St Vith. By 23 December, as the units from St Vith passed through the 508th's positions, the 82nd Airborne was under pressure from three SS divisions plus additional German troops. To make matters worse, the US 3rd Armored Division, which should have been holding the positions on the 82nd's right flank, had pulled out, thus leaving the paratroopers in an extremely exposed position.

Though the situation was tenuous, Gavin ordered his men to hold throughout the night of 23/24 December, while he pleaded for reinforcements. Finally, at 07.00 hours on 24 December, Combat Command B of the 9th Armored Division was assigned, thus giving Gavin some mobile punch to deploy on his threatened right flank.

At 13.30 hours on 24 December, the division received orders to withdraw to more compact defensive positions, though the All Americans found the idea of withdrawing in the face of the enemy anathema. Nevertheless, on Christmas Eve they began withdrawing and by daylight on Christmas Day were occupying new positions extending from south of Trois Ponts through Fosse, Reharmont, Bra, and on to Manhay. Paratroopers being paratroopers, no doubt those occupying positions around Bra managed to find substantial humor in the situation.

The Germans continued to probe the 82nd's new positions and, on the night of 27 December, the 9th SS Panzer Division launched an all-out assault, which was repulsed with great difficulty by the 504th and 508th Parachute Infantry. This seemed to mark the last real threat against the 82nd's positions, however, as the German offensive ran out of impetus due to ever increasing resistance and tenuous supply lines. On 26 December, too, Patton's 3rd Army had broken through to Bastogne thus lifting the siege and scoring a major actual and symbolic victory against Von Rundstedt's forces.

Beginning on 3 January 1945, the US 1st Army went over to the counterattack, with the 82nd Airborne augmented by the hard-driving tankers of the 740th Tank Battalion overrunning the 62nd Volksgrenadier Division and the 9th SS Panzer Division on the first day, taking some two thousand four hundred prisoners in the process. In addition to the 740th's tankers, who matched the paratroopers in aggressiveness, thus winning their respect, the 82nd were augmented by the addition of the 551st Parachute Battalion and the 517th Parachute Infantry Regiment for the counterthrust.

Despite their initial success, the slowness of other units, which lacked the paratroopers' drive, kept the All Americans in check until 8 January when the 82nd was allowed to continue their advance. Pushing on through Vielsalm and to the Salm River, the All Americans re-took the territory they had been forced to relinquish just a couple of weeks before. During the drive, First Sergeant Leonard Funk of the 508th Parachute Infantry won a Congressional Medal of Honor when he used his Thompson SMG to kill a group of Germans attempting to take himself and other paratroopers prisoner. Once at the Salm, the 82nd Airborne was relieved by the 75th Infantry Division and pulled back about 20 miles (30 km) behind the lines until sent back into combat on 28 January.

Along with the 1st Infantry Division, the 82nd now led the assault on the Siegfried Line, beginning on 28 January. A few days later at 04.00 hours on 2 February, the All Americans, led by the 325th Glider Infantry and the 504th Parachute Infantry, drove through 2 miles (3km) of 'dragon's teeth' tank obstacles and seized or destroyed German pillboxes, usually with the 504th's captured Panzerfausts, to punch through the vaunted

Siegfried Line. Once through what the Germans called the 'West Wall,' the 82nd took control of the German towns of Udenbreth and Neuhof and the Hertserott Heights.

After being pulled out of the line for a few days of refitting, the All Americans were back in combat during the push through the Huertgen Forest on 8 February. The 82nd attacked through Kommerscheidt and then drove into Schmidt before pushing on towards the Roer River. Ready to carry out an assault crossing of the Roer, the 82nd was pulled out on 17 February, having helped to blunt the German Ardennes Offensive and then push the enemy back into Germany.

Though used as 'leg' infantry during the Battle of the Bulge, American paratroopers, including the men of the 82nd Airborne, had proven their courage and tenacity once again. As a result of the key blocking positions occupied and held by the paratroopers until the Allied heavier forces could turn the tide, the Germans suffered two hundred and twenty thousand casualties and lost one thousand four hundred armored vehicles which were irreplaceable at this stage of the war. Hitler's great gamble had proven disastrous; the paratroopers and glider riders of the 82nd Airborne were now ready to move in for the kill.

Members of the 2/504th march towards the front lines at Cheneux, Belgium, during the Battle of the Bulge. (*US Army*)

8 THE ALL AMERICAN ROAD TO BERLIN

After their stalwart service during the Battle of the Bulge, the All Americans were pulled back to Sissone once again. Troopers were furloughed, losses were replaced and equipment was brought back up to standard. During this period, the jump on Berlin was given very serious consideration as part of Operation ECLIPSE, the plan for the final defeat and occupation of Germany. On 20 November 1944, Gen Lewis Brereton in command of the 1st Allied Airborne Army, had received orders to plan for an airborne assault against Berlin.

The plan which emerged would have employed two US airborne divisions – including the 82nd – and a British airborne brigade. According to the plan, the 82nd would drop two regiments south of Tempelhof airport. These regiments would then move to block German reinforcements while a third regiment seized the airfield and linked up with other paratroopers around Berlin. Despite the extreme secrecy of the planning, by March, the

Members of the 505th Parachute Infantry who have just made an opposed crossing of the Elbe River link up with British Airborne troops on the other side in late April 1945. (*US Army*)

82nd was carrying out practice assaults on an abandoned airfield near Sissone. One important lesson learned from these run throughs was that removing cargo from Tempelhof's runways during the airlift was likely to be a problem.

Though the Berlin plan was still germinating, late in March after the Rhine crossings, which had included a jump by the US 17th Airborne Division, the All Americans were moved up to the Rhine near Cologne. Among other duties there, the 82nd took charge of a large number of Russian slave laborers who had been relocated by the Germans. The paratroopers first encountered the 'evils' of fraternization with German girls on a large scale near Cologne as well. According to Gen Gavin in his book *On to Berlin*, the paratroopers and glidermen of the 82nd felt they had the perfect solution to the worries about fraternization. The tough combat veterans felt as long as they kept on their airborne caps and jump boots 'as tokens of their patriotism' while 'associating' with local frauleins, fraternization would not be a problem.

Now, 82nd dispositions included the 504th Parachute Infantry north of Cologne and the 505th Parachute Infantry south of Cologne. Although the division was not really charged with taking offensive action at this point,

82nd Airborne trooper guarding Wobelein Concentration Camp which was liberated by the All Americans. (*US Army*)

Sergeant of the 505th Parachute Infantry raises the US flag over a castle in Germany being used as an HQ by the regiment. (*US Army*)

the paratroopers could not resist carrying out aggressive night patrols across the Rhine. Troopers of the 82nd also patroled Cologne and the surrounding area for 'Werewolves,' the supposed German hardcore resistance movement. Although the men of the 82nd had proven during the Battle of the Bulge and earlier that they could live under harsh conditions, they also showed the typical paratrooper's ability to improvise, finding comfortable quarters within Cologne. Company E, 325th Glider Infantry, for example, took up residence in a German candy factory.

Though the men of the 82nd were ready for more action, Gavin was ordered not to let his men be too aggressive since 82nd casualties were to be held to a minimum. What Gavin did not know was that the reason the 82nd was being saved was that they were earmarked to carry out a combat jump against the Japanese mainland, a jump that was likely to entail extremely heavy casualties.

By 28 March, the decision had been taken to drive towards the south to smash the supposed, 'Alpine Redoubt' where the Nazis were expected to make their last stand. As a result, the assault on Berlin was abandoned. The patrols launched across the Rhine by the All Americans were becoming more aggressive in the meantime. On 6 April, for example, a company of

Members of the 505th Parachute Infantry relax in the German castle being used as their HQ. (*US Army*)

the 504th Parachute Infantry crossed the Rhine and occupied the town of Hitdorf, which they held for almost twenty-four hours with the help of another company which crossed to reinforce them. After fighting off heated German counterattacks supported by Tiger tanks, the men of the 504th finally pulled back, having killed an estimated two hundred Germans in the process. In fact, so many Germans had been pulled from other positions along the Rhine to dislodge the two companies of paratroopers that American forces broke through the weakened defenses 13 miles (21km) away.

On 29 April, the 82nd moved to the Elbe with the mission of crossing and then driving on towards Lübeck. At 01.00 hours on 30 April, an assault force of the 505th Parachute Infantry caught the Germans by surprise, surging across the Rhine, to be followed by the 504th Parachute Infantry. On 1 May, with troopers of the 505th riding on tanks of the 740th tank Battalion – old friends of the All Americans from the Battle of the Bulge – the 82nd pushed deeper into German territory. The tankers were astonished to see a substantial number of paratroopers during this advance mounted on horses ranging ahead of the tanks acting as the 505th Parachute Cavalry Regiment.

By 2 May, the troopers of the 82nd were encountering ever increasing

Brig Gen Ira Swift, Asst 82nd Airborne CO, prepares to make a test jump over Tempelhof Field in Berlin during August 1945. While in Berlin on occupation duty, the 82nd was frequently called upon to make demonstration jumps, to some extent at least to demonstrate American might to the Russians. (*US Army*)

numbers of Germans wanting to surrender to avoid capture by the Russians. As a result, on 3 May, the 82nd became the first single division in American military history to take the surrender of an entire army. The paratroopers were astonished by the numbers involved as an estimated one hundred and fifty thousand troops and more than two thousand vehicles of the German 21st Army Group were surrendered to them. The first week in May also saw the liberation of Wobelein concentration camp by the All Americans, who, like other Allied troops who encountered the camps, were disgusted by the inhumanity which confronted them. As a result, the officers had no compunction about forcing the town officials of nearby Ludwigslust to dig graves and prepare crosses for the dead in the camp and then forcing the entire population of the town to view the bodies and attend a ceremony for the dead.

When the war in Europe ended at midnight on the night of 8/9 May, the 82nd Airborne had established a combat record unsurpassed in the US Army. During the war, sixty thousand men had served in the division, which had spent 422 days in combat in six countries. Of those days, 157 of them had resulted directly from airborne deployment. A total of 3,228 All

Maj Gen Gavin prepares for a test jump on Tempelhof in August 1945. Note the good view offered of the paratrooper boots. (*US Army*)

Americans had either been killed in action or died later of their wounds. Awards for gallantry won by members of the division included four Congressional Medals of Honor, twenty-eight Distinguished Service Crosses, one Distinguished Service Medal, thirty-two Legion of Merits, 894 Silver Stars and 2,478 Bronze Stars, not to mention numerous foreign awards.

The Master Race now vanquished, the 82nd was pulled back to France once again to receive replacements prior to occupation duty in Berlin. At this point many of the 82nd veterans of Sicily, Italy, Normandy, Holland, and Germany had well over the eighty-five points needed to rotate home and thus they left the division. However, they were frequently replaced by other combat veterans of the 17th and 101st Airborne Divisions who now joined the All Americans, though retaining their 'Screaming Eagle' or 'Talon From Heaven' patches with justifiable pride on their right shoulders to indicate combat with these divisions.

At the specific request of both the Soviet and British occupying powers, the 82nd was moved from Epinal, France, in July just after the Potsdam Conference, to join the British 6th Armoured Division and the Soviet 5th Cossack Division in occupying Berlin. As a result, Maj Gen Gavin became the senior US officer in Berlin and thus served on the *Kommandantura*, which

governed the occupied city. Among the first priorities faced by the 82nd
and the other occupying units in Berlin was cleaning up the thousands of
bodies remaining from the final battle for the city, especially the more than
three thousand in the subways. Food and fuel also had to be distributed to
the population as winter approached.

Gavin found working with the Soviets increasingly difficult as they
grew ever more truculent, complaining about such things as the criticism
of Soviet atrocities in Berlin in the American press. However, the Soviets
soon learned that the tough airborne troopers of the 82nd could not be
intimidated. In at least one instance, a Soviet soldier drew a pistol on one
of the All Americans who promptly shot the Red soldier. Gavin backed his
men on this and other incidents to the hilt, his and the All Americans' tough
stand gaining the grudging respect of the Soviet troops.

While occupying Berlin, the 82nd found it had many prominent visitors,
among the earliest ones being Gen Eisenhower and Marshal Zhukov of the
Soviet Union. Gavin was impressed with Zhukov.

Because of the number of important visitors, including droves of US
Congressmen, the 82nd organised an impressive Honor Guard Company

In August 1945, Marshal Georgi Zhukov and the US Senate Foreign Relations Committee
review the 82nd Airborne in Berlin. Maj Gen Gavin is wearing the side cap. (*US Army*)

Honor Guard of the 82nd Airborne as flags of USA, Great Britain, Soviet Union, and France are raised at the court house where the Germans who attempted to assassinate Hitler were tried. (*US Army*)

of highly decorated combat veterans, all over six feet tall. Immaculate in white parachute silk scarves, white gloves and white shoelaces, the All American Honor Guard, drilled to perfection, never failed to impress visitors with their turnout.

Despite the 82nd's legendary combat record, Gavin was informed in October 1945 that the 82nd was to be disbanded. As a result, Gavin began an informal lobbying effort to find support in Washington for keeping the 82nd Airborne as the post-war US airborne division. By late November, Gavin's efforts as well as those of other admirers of the All Americans had borne fruit as it was decided that the 82nd would remain in existence as the post-war US airborne division. Not only that but the 82nd would return to the United States shortly after the beginning of 1946 to stage a victory parade down New York's Fifth Avenue.

The response of the crowd in New York was outstanding as the proud paratroopers, 'Slim Jim' Gavin at their front as he had always been in combat, marched through the streets of Manhattan. The men who had written the first chapters of the magnificent combat history of the 82nd Airborne Division with their sweat and blood were now marching home to much-deserved glory. Some of them had found they liked the Army and would stay around to help write the chapters still to come, while the sons, grandsons and – most recently – the granddaughters of some of those World War Two All Americans would attempt to fill the jump boots of those who had bailed out into combat against the Germans and Italians.

9 POST-WAR STRATEGIC RESERVE

After their triumphant victory parade down Fifth Avenue in New York City, the troopers of the 82nd Airborne received a much deserved furlough before the division returned to its permanent home at Fort Bragg. During the post-war years, it would become the keystone of the United States' strategic reserve. Ironically, the fact that the 82nd was so combat ready and so critical to the Joint Chiefs' contingency planning frequently kept the division from being committed to combat—for instance, during the Korean War—while far less combat ready divisions were sent into action. Although the fate of airborne divisions and specifically the 82nd had been somewhat in question at the end of the war, the All Americans' future became assured in 1948 as the division became part of the regular US Army.

The relevance of the airborne arm in the post-war Army was hotly debated in the pages of *Infantry Journal* during the immediate years after

In November 1949, Brig Gen Charles Canham, commanding officer of the 82nd Airborne speaks to the division at Fort Bragg. (*US Army*)

the war, with 82nd CO Maj Gen James Gavin the primary spokesman and theorist of airborne forces. There were even serious suggestions that the entire post-war US Army should be parachute trained to lend versatility and mobility. Even airborne horse cavalry was suggested in the July 1946 issue of *Military Revue*. In the January, 1948, issue of *Infantry Journal*, Gavin gave support to the suggestion that fast moving reconnaissance elements should be air transportable, but he was primarily stressing that all armored vehicles and artillery should be capable of being transported by air. It was a revolutionary idea in the days before the C-141 and other mammoth transports, though Gavin did point out that the B-36 bomber could be converted to transport M4 Sherman tanks. Realizing, like the Soviets, that airborne forces needed an armored vehicle of their own to counter the threat from enemy armor, Gavin pressed for the development of a lightly-armored vehicle of about five tons with a 'highly penetrative' gun able to knock out heavy tanks up to about two thousand five hundred yards. Tactically, Gavin presented an excellent argument for the vertical envelopment possibilities of inserting a tank force directly into the enemy rear.

Members of the 82nd Airborne loading their equipment aboard a C-119 transport aircraft prior to 'Exercise Swarmer' in April 1950. Note the Browning water-cooled machine gun still in use at left foreground. (*USAF*)

The 82nd in the 1950s

With the beginning of the Korean War in June 1950, the Unites States armed forces found themselves stretched very thinly as units were rushed to Korea, while the credibility of the commitment to block a Soviet move into Western Europe had to be maintained with powerful units in Europe. In July 1950, Gen Douglas MacArthur requested the release of a regimental combat team from the 82nd for use in Korea, and serious consideration was given during the next month to committing the entire 82nd Airborne to Korea. By late 1950, it was understood that the 82nd could deploy to Korea within thirty days if necessary, and in December, consideration was given to moving the 82nd to Japan to be more readily available should the situation deteriorate to the point that they were needed rapidly.

However, the 82nd was virtually the only combat ready division remaining in the strategic reserve by the fall of 1951; hence, while other units in the United States were denuded of infantry battalions for Korea, the 82nd was spared. When planning for 'Operation CHROMITE, the flanking operation against the North Koreans at Inchon, Gen MacArthur

In June 1950, members of the 307th Airborne Engineers load a bulldozer aboard a C-119 transport. (*US Army*)

Members of the 82nd Airborne recover a jeep which has been dropped by parachute during
'Exercise Cold Spot' in February 1953. (*USAF*)

wanted a regimental combat team from the 82nd but instead received
the 187th Regimental Combat Team from the 11th Airborne. Though the
187th arrived too late for the Inchon landings in September 1950 they did
make two combat jumps during the war and would later join the 82nd for
a period during the 1950s.

In the late 1940s and early 1950s, life in the 82nd Airborne consisted
primarily of intensive training from Alaska to Panama and in the Far
East as well as all over the continental US interspersed with ceremonial
duties in parades or demonstrations. Among the exercises during the early
and mid-1950s were LONG HORN in Texas in 1952, SNOW STORY at Camp
Drum, New York, in 1953, SAGE BRUSH at Fort Polk, Louisiana, in 1955,
and ARCTIC NIGHT in Greenland in 1956.

Re-organization, 1957–8

For the first decade after the war, the division's organization had undergone some gradual changes. Glider infantry, for example, had been phased
out to be replaced entirely by parachute infantry. However, in 1957–8,
a major re-organization was undertaken under the Pentomic system, a
system devised particularly for nuclear warfare under which an army

division was subdivided into five battle groups. After this re-organization, the 82nd consisted of five airborne battle groups plus ancillary units.

82nd Airborne Division, 1958

Airborne Infantry Battle Groups
    1/325th, 1/504th*, 1/505th*, 2/501th, 2/503th Parachute Infantry

Divisional Artillery
    A/319th, B/319th, C/319th, D/320th, E/320th, B/377th
    Airborne Batteries

Support Group
    HQ and HQ Company
    Division Band
    782nd Maintenance Battalion
    82nd Quartermaster Parachute Supply and Maintenance Company
    407th Supply and Transportation Company
    82nd Medical Company

Separate Units
    82nd Aviation Company
    Troop A/17th Cavalry
    82nd Signal Battalion
    307th Engineer Battalion

*In 1958, the 1/187th and 2/504th replaced the 1/505th and 1/504th respectively.

STRAC

In 1958, the XVIIIth Airborne Corps was designated the Strategic Army Corps, thus originating the term 'STRAC' which was often used to describe the airborne troops and to indicate smartness and combat readiness. While the original meaning of the term has become obscured, the term remains in the jargon of the XVIIIth Airborne Corps today, though defined on the corps sign at Fort Bragg as standing for: Skilled, Tough, Ready Around the Clock. Intended for immediate deployment to any trouble spot, the Strategic Army Corps initially designated the 101st Airborne as the spearhead unit for the corps, ready to go into immediate action, followed rapidly by the All Americans.

Two major exercises in 1959 tested the 82nd's readiness for rapid deployment. In February, 1,600 men of the division equipped with Honest John rockets were airlifted to Panama for jungle training as part of BANYAN TREE. In October and November, the 82nd joined with the 101st Airborne and the 4th Infantry Division in a major test of STRAC's readiness.

Although John F. Kennedy is thought of primarily as a patron of the Special Forces, the youthful President also appreciated the panache

Members of the 82nd Airborne board their C-119 transport prior to being dropped in 'Exercise Cold Spot' during February 1953. (*USAF*)

of the 82nd Airborne Division who marched in his inaugural parade on 20 January 1961. The President later reviewed the division at Pope Air Force Base in October 1961. The next year, during the Cuban Missile Crisis, it appeared as if the 82nd might be sent into combat by the President as elements of the division were chuted up and ready to drop over Cuba if needed to enforce the President's ultimatum to the Soviet Union.

Re-organization, 1964
In May 1964, the 82nd Airborne was re-organised again, now under the ROAD system which instituted the battalion and brigade alignment. As of this 1964 re-organization, the division consisted of three brigades, plus ancillary units.

82nd Airborne Division, 1964

1st Brigade
    1/504th, 2/504th, 2/508th Parachute Infantry Battalions
2nd Brigade
    1/325th, 2/325th, 3/325th Parachute Infantry Battalions

3rd Brigade
   1/505th, 2/505th, 1/508th Parachute Infantry Battalions

Divisional Artillery
   1/319th, 1/320th, 2/321th Airborne Artillery Battalions

Division Support Command
   HQ, HQ Company and Band
   782nd Maintenance Battalion
   307th Medical Battalion
   407th Supply and Transport Battalion
   82nd Administrative Company

Separate Units
   82nd Aviation Battalion
   307th Engineer Battalion
   82nd Signal Battalion
   1/17th Cavalry
   82nd Military Intelligence Company
   82nd Military Police Company

In April 1965, the division's readiness and new organization were tested when the battalions were deployed to the Dominican Republic to intervene in that country's civil war. The All American units remained committed there for the next seventeen months, as described in the next chapter.

TO&E, 1967

The 82nd Airborne Division of the 1960s was an extremely formidable unit, well organised and well trained. At this point, reference to a detailed breakdown of the Table of Organization and Equipment (TO&E) of the 82nd Airborne Division in 1967 (under the ROAD system of 1964) will be useful, illustrating the changes which had taken place during the first quarter century of America's premier airborne division. (See pp178–83)

Totalling about thirteen thousand five hundred men according to its 1967 TO&E, the 82nd Airborne underwent further changes and increases in size and capability. The 502nd Support Company joined the division in 1968, while the 407th Supply and Transport Battalion was eliminated. In June 1969, the 4th Battalion/68th Armor joined the division from Fort Riley, Kansas. Then, in December 1970, the 7th Battalion (Airborne)/60th Artillery (Air Defense) was added, equipped with the lethal 30mm six-barrel rotary cannon. In 1972, this latter battalion was redesignated the 3rd Battalion (Airborne)/14th Air Defense Artillery. The manpower of these units pushed the division closer to its current strength of sixteen thousand troopers.

As protests against the Vietnam War grew and as racial unrest fomented riots in major American cities, the 82nd Airborne found itself reluctantly

Air Force weather expert and members of the 82nd Airborne take wind velocity readings during 'Operation Cold Spot' in February 1953. (*USAF*)

committed to internal security duties. The first major deployment on anti-riot duty was to Detroit on 24 July 1967 where the 3rd Brigade remained until 5 August 1967, helping to restore law and order. Then, on 19 October 1967, the 1st Brigade was sent to Washington DC for four days to help quell civil disturbances. Finally, on 6 April 1968, a reinforced brigade of the 82nd was sent to Washington once again to help put down rioting.

At that point, only one brigade of the 82nd remained in reserve as the 3rd Brigade had been rushed to the Republic of Vietnam on 13 February 1968 to help to blunt the Tet Offensive. Initially, consideration had been given to sending the entire division, but the threat of even broader rioting in US cities and the need to retain the division in the strategic reserve pre-empted the commitment of more than one brigade to south-east Asia. In fact, to bring the division back up to strength, a 4th Brigade was formed to replace the 3rd while it was in Vietnam.

In evaluating the use of All American paratroopers to patrol the streets of black ghettos in American cities with fixed bayonets, a key point to bear in mind is that the 82nd at this point contained a substantial percentage of tough, dedicated black paratroopers – so many that a joke current around Fort Bragg in the 1960s was that the 'AA' on the division shoulder sleeve insignia stood for 'All African.' The sight of fellow blacks with bloused trousers in spit-shined paratrooper boots serving in the highly respected 82nd Airborne Division was probably less inflammatory than the presence of the National Guard and local police, both of which, justly or unjustly, were viewed as racist. Though they may not have liked the urban security assignment the troopers of the 82nd Airborne – black and white – carried out their mission.

Their participation in Field Training Exercise FOCUS RETINA was more in line with their mission as the keystone of the strategic reserve. On 21 March 1969, the 82nd's 2nd Brigade plus attached elements jumped into Korea as the culmination of the longest airborne operation in history.

The 82nd in the 1970s and 1980s

Throughout the 1970s, the All Americans continued their cycle of training and readiness exercises. Various battalions carried out long distance exercises such as FREEDOM VAULT to Korea by the 2/504th, DEEP FURROW to Turkey by the 1/325th, and DEEP FURROW 72 to Greece by the 2/505th. During the 1970s, also, the division was alerted for two major combat operations to rescue civilians. In May 1978, division ready elements

During 'Exercise Devil Arrow' in September 1962, members of the 82nd Airborne Division carry out a counter-guerrilla operation against 'guerrillas' from the 5th and 7th Special Forces Groups and the 22nd SAS Regiment. (*US Army*)

were alerted for a possible drop at Kolwezi in Zaire where Katangan rebels were murdering European civilians, but, while the US government under Jimmy Carter pondered this commitment, France's 2nd Foreign Legion Parachute Regiment made their now legendary combat jump at Kolwezi instead of the All Americans. Then, in November 1979, the division was alerted once again, this time for a possible jump to free the American hostages in Teheran. Once again, however, political rather than military considerations won out, and the All Americans stood down rather than jumping over Iran. Should any reader have any doubt about enthusiasm among the troopers of the 82nd for such an operation, it should be noted that when graduates of jump school at this period were asked to fill out their 'dream sheets' requesting the location of their next assignment they almost universally put Iran, indicating their desire to jump in and kill followers of the Ayatollah!

In 1982, the All Americans, the USA's most combat ready fighting division, were assigned as peacekeepers in the Gaza Strip, the 1/505th being sent in March. That part of the Middle East being rather volatile, tough combat troops make the best peacekeepers, though, and the troopers got a chance to enhance their desert training. Henceforth, while

During 'Exercise Sunshade IV' in January 1953, members of the 503rd Airborne Battle Group take part in a live-fire exercise. (*US Army*)

the peacekeeping mission lasted, each six months a battalion of the 82nd would alternate with one from the 101st Airborne in the Sinai. Troopers of the 82nd had also jumped into Egypt during 1981 as part of the BRIGHT STAR exercise with the Egyptians. In 1982, two thousand All Americans jumped as part of GALLANT EAGLE II in a major Rapid Deployment Force exercise and another 1,870 into West Germany as part of the REFORGER 82 NATO exercise.

During 1983, the division's first combat commitment in almost twenty years took place to the island of Grenada. The 1980s have also seen the division's re-organization along the Army's regimental system.

On 17 March 1988, it appeared as if troopers of the 82nd might be going into action as they were deployed to Palmerola Air Base in Honduras following an incursion by Nicaraguan troops into that country in pursuit of Contra rebels. In actuality, the two battalions of the 82nd supported by two further battalions of the 7th Light Infantry were sent on a 'readiness exercise' to send a message to Nicaragua. The proximity of the tough troopers of the 82nd was meant to signal US support for Honduras and the Contras and served its purpose as the Nicaraguan forces withdrew back across the border into their own territory. Their mission accomplished, and the rapid deployment ability of the 82nd's ready forces tested once again, the paratroopers returned to Fort Bragg, one battalion parachuting 'home' onto Sicily Drop Zone on 28 March.

The 82nd Airborne today continues its training regimen of realistic and rigorous training (as many as ten paratroopers of the division have died in parachuting accidents in a recent year) as it keeps its weapons and skills honed for the next time the division is sent into action.

10 'POWER PACK'

During the spring of 1965, the All Americans were going about their normal rigorous training schedule designed to keep the division combat ready. As the end of April approached, the division was preparing for a 'Blue Chip' demonstration drop before a large number of spectators. As usual, the Division Ready Battalion, in this case the 1/508th had to be prepared for immediate deployment to any trouble spot, yet few in the 1/508th realized that at 00.15 hours on 27 April 1965 the alert raising their state of readiness to 'Defcon 3' was anything more than another practice alert. In fact, the 82nd Airborne was about to go into combat. About 19.30 hours on 28 April, the status of the 1/508th was raised to 'Defcon 2' indicating the likelihood of imminent action.

The reason for the alert was the civil war raging in the Dominican Republic which was to cost a thousand lives during its first week. Not only was the Republic considered important to US national security under the Monroe Doctrine, but the bloody civil war was also threatening US civilians at the embassy and elsewhere in the strife-torn country. With American interests threatened, the 82nd Airborne became an important instrument of national policy and had thus to be ready for rapid deployment.

The 82nd's support elements had been busily rigging heavy equipment for a combat jump over the Dominican Republic, 111 planes having been rigged for heavy drop and thirty-three for troop drop, when at 19.30 hours on 29 April, the All Americans received orders to deploy to the Caribbean. Initially, the plan called for the intervention forces, codenamed 'Power Pack,' to stopover in Puerto Rico and then make a parachute assault. However, while en route orders were changed and the initial assault elements were ordered to go directly in to San Isidro Airport.

As a result, at 01.30 hours on 30 April, the first C-130 carrying troopers of the 1/508th touched down, to be followed over the next three hours by the remaining thirty-two planes carrying the initial elements of the All Americans. Additional increments would continue to come in over the next few days as first the 3rd Brigade, then the remaining brigades would arrive. The 1/505th less Company C which was attached to the 1/508th was assigned the mission of securing the airfield for the follow up elements of the division.

Meanwhile, the 1/508th augmented by Company C, 1/505th and elements of the 1/17th Cavalry and 307th Engineers moved out as rapidly as possible towards the Duarte bridge with orders to seize it. As the paratroopers approached the bridge, many heard hostile fire for the first time as they

Member of the 82nd Airborne on patrol in the Dominican Republic. (*US Army*)

began to take sniper fire. Throughout the day on 30 April, these advance elements of the 82nd cleared the bridge and river banks of the enemy. Company C of the 1/505th drew a particularly tough assignment as they had to clear enemy snipers from the power plant which supplied the capital city of Santo Domingo, just across the river. Using well-practiced building clearing tactics, the men of the 505th soon secured the critical power plant, allowing their comrades to drive on across the bridge and begin to clear the capital city itself. Using their 106mm recoilless rifles for fire support, the men of Company C, 1/505th, held the power plant and interdicted rebel movement on the river for the next few days. By the end of 30 April, the All Americans not only controled the bridge over the Ozama River and its banks but had cleared a six block radius of the city itself in preparation for driving on towards the American Embassy the next day. During the process, however, casualties had been taken from snipers' fire.

At 09.00 hours the next morning, 1 May, the 1/508th received orders to form a task force to thrust across the city to link up with the US Marines of the Caribbean ready force which had been lifted ashore by helicopters between 28 and 30 April to protect American civilians and reinforce the Marine contingent at the US Embassy. Two platoons, including the battalion recon platoon, pushed across the city, eliminating enemy resistance when encountered and linking up with the Marines at 13.15 hours. In the process, the 1/508th suffered one trooper killed in action, the first 82nd KIA since the end of World War Two.

Making use of their mobility, Troop A/17th Cavalry carried out patrols along the banks of the Ozama River during the early days of May helping to ferret the rebels out of positions from which they could snipe at the paratroopers moving across the Duarte bridge.

Having spearheaded the move into Santo Domingo, the 1/508th was relieved on 2 May by the 1/505th, though Company A of the 1/508th remained to provide security for the Duarte bridge so that the follow-on contingents could move through without hesitation. The remainder of the 1/508th assumed positions around San Isidro Airport to provide perimeter security for the C-130s still arriving with additional elements of the division and supplies.

Almost immediately upon moving into the 'frontlines' the 1/505th began breaking up bands of looters and setting up roadblocks. The roadblocks included one in rebel-controled territory which the rebels singled out for special attention, raining sniper fire on it. Later, a hostile crowd of over one thousand people advanced on the roadblock trying to goad the All Americans manning it into firing into them, thus creating instant martyrs. Instead, however, they found themselves facing cold-eyed paratroopers advancing on them with fixed bayonets and soon dispersed. During the next couple of days, the 1/505th improved their positions and were joined on 2 May by the 2/505th, which had arrived at San Isidro the previous day. The 2/505th moved across the Duarte bridge and along the 'All American Expressway,' a corridor now held by the 82nd through the city. On the morning of 3 May, the 2/505th began house-to-house clearing operations along the corridor and also began distributing food and medical aid to the local population.

The 2/325th had arrived on 1 May and on 2 May had taken over security for San Isidro. However, at 24.00 hours on 2 May, the troopers of the 2/325th launched an attack across the Santo Domingo which opened the 'All American Expressway' to the Marine positions. The 1/325th began arriving at San Isidro on the afternoon of 2 May and by 3 May was prepared to go into action wherever needed. The 3/325th also arrived on 2 May and on 3 May moved to secure the eastern bank of the Ozama River, dealing with snipers and infiltrators both ashore and in small boats on the river.

Perhaps the 82nd's most famous regiment, the 504th Parachute Infantry – the 'Devils in Baggy Pants' – arrived on 3 May in the form of the 1/504th and 2/504th. The 1/504th was assigned security positions around the division command post, while the 2/504th and the 2/508th, also arriving on 3 May, were ordered to be ready to go into action as needed.

Artillery units of the division had begun arriving during the first few days and were prepared to give fire support to the infantry if needed, having sent Forward Observers along with the infantry battalions moving into Santo Domingo. Due to the concentration of civilians in the city and the fact that the rebels encountered lacked heavy weapons, no high

May 1965, bandsmen of the 82nd Airborne Division march through the streets of Santo Domingo. (*US Army*)

explosive fire had been called for, but the gunners had fired illumination rounds during night operations.

Lead elements of the 82nd Signal Battalion had come in with the first planeloads of the 1/508th to establish a communications link with the naval forces off shore. Then, by 2 May, troopers of the Signal Battalion had helped to establish communications with the Marines at the embassy by helilifting a communications hut onto the roof of a building across from the embassy.

During these first days, while the infantry battalions had been securing portions of the city, the men of the 307th Engineers had drawn the unenviable task of beginning to clear trash from the streets of Santo Domingo and of restoring the water supply, often taking snipers' fire in the process. Being not just combat engineers, but airborne combat engineers, the troopers of the 307th were able to deal quite effectively with the snipers when encountered.

Rejoined by Company A, which had been securing the Duarte bridge, the 1/505th sent out a motorized patrol in coordination with the Dominican armed forces based at the International Airport. Then, on 5 May, the 1/505th was withdrawn to positions in the countryside on the east bank of the Ozama River. Relieved by the 1/325th on 4 May, the 2/505th assumed security duties for the divisional command post on 5 May.

The 1/325th had moved into action on 4 May when the battalion replaced the 2/505th guarding the Line of Communication to the US Embassy, also known as the 'Corridor' or the 'All American Expressway'. The 325th's other two battalions, the 2/325th and 3/325th, also helped secure the corridor and over the next weeks helped to expand it into former rebel-held territory.

By 4 May, the All Americans had been given vertical mobility as the 82nd Aviation Battalion had arrived with over twenty-five helicopters. In addition to troop lift, the aviation battalion would offer aerial recon, medevac and other support services. Helicopters capable of delivering CS gas were also on call if needed to quell large civil disturbances, as were gunships.

On 5 May, the 1/504th was relieved of security duties by the 2/505th moving forward towards Santo Domingo. Then, on 6 May, the 1/504th carried out a search and clear mission against the village of Calero. The 2/508th had been ordered to secure the east bank of the Ozama River south of the Duarte bridge and bridge itself as of 4 May. While carrying out their mission, the troopers of the 2/508th took fire from snipers, including some aboard the ship *Santo Domingo* which they quickly silenced with a single 106mm recoilless rifle round.

Throughout these operations during the first week in May, the 1/17th Cavalry provided escorts to convoys moving along the corridor and motorized patrols along the banks of the Ozama. Like the other All Americans, however, the cavalrymen had problems adjusting to their relatively passive

82nd Airborne checkpoint in the Dominican Republic. (*US Army*)

role; the paratroopers knew they could handle the rebels quickly and effectively if turned loose to 'Kick ass and take names,' but while negotiations were going on they were restricted to security duties.

Making use of the air mobility provided by the 82nd Aviation Battalion, elements of the 1/508th carried out heliborne reconnaissance missions. On 9 May, the recon platoon of the 1/508th escorted 120 Americans from the Ambassador Hotel to San Isidro Airport for evacuation. Then, from 9 to 11 May, the 1/508th became the division ready force.

On 9 May, the 1/505th was pulled back to handle security duties at San Isidro, but Company C was detached to guard the US Embassy. Another company of the 1/505th – Company A – drew an even more interesting assignment, being detailed to keep the Dominican air force on the ground so it could not intervene while the USA was trying to workout a negotiated settlement. The 2/505th also drew security duties, being assigned to protect the division CP until 10 May.

Between 4 and 11 May, the 1/325th helped extend the corridor and provide security along it. Both the 2/325th and 3/325th also provided security along the corridor until being ordered to patrol and secure the east bank of the Ozama River on 8 May. The 2/325th and 3/325th had been relieved by the 1/504th and 2/504th along the corridor, and the 'Devils in Baggy Pants' engaged rebels in the Voice of Santo Domingo Radio and TV building in heavy firefights while establishing their hegemony over the corridor. The 2/508th also assumed critical duties along the 'All American Expressway' on 8 May, taking responsibility for checkpoints controling traffic into and out of rebel held areas.

As the All Americans completed their second week in the Dominican Republic and moved into their third, they settled into the routine of internal security. As assault troops, they would have preferred to go in and eliminate the rebel threat permanently, but as professionals they did their job. Not only did they perform their military job well, but the tough paratroopers proved surprisingly effective at a 'hearts and minds' campaign as they distributed food and gave medical aid.

Between 11 and 21 May, the 1/508th moved to the east side of the Ozama River where they came under enemy fire an average of twenty times per day, though through the effective use of their 106mm recoilless rifles they made the rebel snipers pay dearly. Beginning on 21 May, the 1/505th re-assumed responsibility for the center area of the corridor, including two key checkpoints.

Due to the effective checkpoints established by the All Americans leading into and out of rebel zones, the rebels had to find other infiltration and exfiltration routes; hence, they began using the sewers to move freely around the city. Once this ruse was discovered by the paratroopers, the 307th Engineers were brought in to map the sewers and then emplace the wire barriers to prevent movement, but the airborne engineers had some point blank firefights with the rebels beneath the city streets in the process.

On 11 May, the 2/505th was attached to the 1st Brigade to begin what would turn out to be thirty-eight days along the Corridor, at one point taking mortar and 37mm tank fire in the process. Between 12 and 31 May, the 1/325th assumed various sentry duties including San Isidro Airport, the port facilities, and the division CP. Beginning on 21 May, the 2/325th took over security responsibilities for the power plant as well as the east bank of the Ozama River. On 21 May also, the 3/325th was attached to the 3rd Brigade to assume responsibility for the western portion of the corridor.

One paratrooper from the 1/504th accounted for three rebel leaders, including one Cuban-trained Communist, with a well-placed 3.5inch rocket on 19 May. But as the month drew to a close, fighting seemed to be dying down. The lack of heavy opposition, in fact, caused some elements of the division to be ordered back to Fort Bragg at the end of May, including divisional artillery and some mortar platoons.

The 1/508th moved back to the area they had cleared as the spearhead of the All American presence on 21 May, remaining along the west bank of the Ozama until 2 June. Then, on 4 June, they added the power plant and Duarte bridge to their responsibilities. To back up the infantry battalions should they be ordered to move against the rebels, the 1/17th Cavalry took positions in the area south of the Duarte bridge, though the cavalry found it difficult to take rebel fire without returning it.

The 2/505th got a chance to host correspondent Dickie Chappell, who was always popular with the paratroopers, in early June. The first days in June also saw the 1/325th and 2/325th relieving the Marines near the US Embassy, but then they were relieved themselves by Brazilian troops of the OAS Peacekeeping Force on 7 June. The situation being relatively stable, various units were pulled back during late May and early June for rest and training.

However, after a political rally on 14 June sponsored by the pro-Castro 14 June Movement, the rebels began to pour heavy fire into 82nd positions on 15 June. As a result, the All Americans finally received orders to move against the rebels. The 1/508th drove south into the rebel area of the city on 15/16 June, suffering thirty casualties but inflicting sixty-seven KIA and 59 WIA (Wounded in Action) against the rebels. Supporting the 1/508th advance was the 1/505th which began its own advance on 15 June, destroying a rebel tank with 106mm fire as well as leveling numerous rebel bunkers with the recoilless rifles. Giving fire support to pin down rebels near their sector was the 2/505th. On 15 June also, the cavalrymen finally got a chance to pay the rebels back for the fire they had been forced to stand by and take as they provided fire support for the advancing infantrymen.

By 17 June, the rebel guns were silenced and the 82nd assumed a defensive posture once again. For the most part, the remainder of the time in the Dominican Republic was spent on security duties along the Corridor and at the US Embassy or in training. Over the remainder of the summer, many of the All Americans returned to Fort Bragg,

82nd Airborne position guarding approach to the Duarte bridge in the Dominican Republic. (*US Army*)

though the 1st Brigade would remain for over a year as part of the peacekeeping force.

While in the Dominican Republic, the 82nd Airborne had suffered sixty casualties but had inflicted many times that number on the enemy. The peacekeeping role had been a frustrating one since the aggressive paratroopers had been held in check and not allowed to deal effectively with the rebels. Nevertheless, the troopers of the 82nd had performed well, proving quite popular with many of the Dominicans, who soon learned to greet them with the paratroopers' catchphrase: 'All the Way!'

The Dominican Republic marked a small but significant combat commitment of the men of the 82nd Airborne. A much larger commitment was on the horizon, however. In fact, while most of the division had been serving in the Dominican Republic, elements of the 82nd Aviation Battalion had been deployed to the Republic of Vietnam.

11 VIETNAM

Although the 82nd Airborne still remained the primary ready strategic reserve in CONUS (Continental United States) during the early stages of the Vietnam War, the consternation caused by the Tet Offensive which had swept across the Republic of Vietnam on 31 January 1968 forced the Joint Chiefs of Staff to deplete even the All Americans in an attempt to avert a perceived disaster in Vietnam. In actuality, Tet proved to be a major military defeat for the Viet Cong but a media defeat for the USA as the American public perceived it as a disaster.

Sending the entire 82nd Airborne Division to Vietnam would have eliminated completely US rapid reinforcement capability in Europe and severely limited options to intervene anywhere else in the world. Furthermore, it was considered necessary to retain the 82nd in the USA to maintain order at home in the wake of riots and anti-war protests. Nevertheless, the 82nd offered the best available pool of immediately deployable, combat ready troops. As a result, the decision was taken to send the 3rd Brigade of the 82nd. The first elements took off for Chu Lai within twenty-four hours of being alerted.

Following Col Alex R. Bolling Jr. the brigade commander, and his staff

Choppers of the 82nd Aviation Battalion provide lift for men of the 173rd Airborne Brigade during operations in the Republic of Vietnam in 1965. (*US Army*)

Scouts from the 82nd Airborne Divison in a jeep armed with an M-60 MG. (*US Army*)

was the remainder of the brigade in 135 C-141s and six C-133s. President Lyndon B. Johnson himself flew in on Air Force One to see the brigade off, at one point answering the enthusiastically shouted 'All the Way, Sir!' of three thousand five hundred paratroopers with the traditional 'Airborne!' Included among the units deployed to Vietnam were the 1/505th, 2/505th, and 1/508th; 82nd Support Battalion; the 58th Signal Company; Company C, 307th Engineer Battalion (Airborne); 2nd Battalion, 321st Artillery (105mm) (Airborne); Troop B, 1st Squadron, 17th Cavalry (Armored); Company O, 75th Ranger; and Company A, 82nd Aviation Battalion. Of the more than three thousand five hundred troops deployed, about eighty per cent had seen previous service in Vietnam with other units, thus making the 3rd Brigade an extremely veteran contingent. However, so rapidly had the deployment taken place that a goodly number of those deployed had only recently returned from Vietnam and were not anxious to go back. As a result, they were given the option of staying or returning to Fort Bragg; 2,513 out of 3,650 chose to return to the division.

The 82nd would, however, retain its strategic rapid deployment mission. Consequently, while the 3rd Brigade was in Vietnam, a 4th Brigade was formed composed of the 3/504th, 3/505th and 4/325th; the 3/320th Artillery; Troop K, 1/17th Cavalry; Company D, 307th Medical Battalion;

In June 1969, a 508th Airborne Infantry officer outlines a forthcoming operation near Trung Lap to the men of his company. Note that from the insignia on the officer's right shoulder he has served a previous tour in Vietnam with the 199th Infantry Brigade. (*US Army*)

and the 596th Engineer Company, 307th Engineer Battalion. These units would remain in existence throughout the 3rd Brigade's commitment to the Republic of Vietnam.

Shortly after their arrival in the country, the troopers of the 82nd were attached to the 101st Airborne Division near Hue-Phu Bai. The 82nd base camp was named Camp Rodriguez after an All American sergeant killed by a booby trap. It was positioned to allow the paratroopers to protect the city of Hue from an enemy thrust from the south. On 9 March 1968, the 82nd came under 101st control and soon joined the Screaming Eagles in Operation CARENTAN which took advantage of the patroling skill and small unit tactics of the paratroopers to deny the enemy freedom of movement at night. All American Hunter-Killer patrols and ambushes soon took a heavy toll of the Communists, who were already reeling from the heavy losses they had suffered during the Tet Offensive. Even before CARENTAN, members of the 82nd had been in combat, on 11 March paratroopers having countered an enemy ambush against a truck convoy near Camp Rodriguez.

After the successes in CARENTAN, the All Americans were used on intelligence gathering missions, in which they uncovered evidence of Viet Cong (VC) atrocities in the area, and on area security missions. Small groups of paratroopers continued to run very effective ambushes as well.

Over the next few months, the troopers of the 82nd took part in various other operations, the most important of which was CARENTAN II along with the 101st Airborne and the Army of the Republic of Vietnam (ARVN) 1st Division. Beginning on 1 April and running until 17 May, this operation in Quang Tri and Thua Thien Provinces would account for two thousand one hundred enemy casualties. By 17 May, when this operation ended, the 3rd Brigade had suffered 313 casualties, including forty-three dead, but had inflicted 727 dead on the enemy and had captured another eighteen. On 1 May, even before the CARENTAN II had ended, the 3rd Brigade, 82nd Airborne, came directly under the control of US Army Vietnam.

Though the All Americans continued to help to secure the area around Hue-Phu Bai for the remainder of the summer, in September 1968, the 3rd Brigade was moved south to help to counter a threat in III Corps to Saigon. In October, they were joined in this mission by the 1st Cavalry Division (Airmobile), thus putting two of the most effective US units in country near the capital. Under the Capital Military Assistance Command,

Members of Company C, 1st Battalion, 508th Airborne Infantry board a C-47 Chinook during operations in Nghia Province in June 1969. (*US Army*)

Members of the 82nd Airborne Division prepare an 81mm mortar for firing during training at Fort Bragg in 1979. (*US Army*)

the All Americans proved especially valuable at countering infiltrators and rocket attacks against Tan Son Nhut Airfield.

To accomplish the missions around Saigon which had been assigned to the 'Golden Brigade' (as the 3rd Brigade, 82nd Airborne, was sometimes known in Vietnam by public relation types, though rarely by the tough paratroopers themselves), Brig Gen George Dickerson, commanding the Brigade since December 1968, ordered his troopers not only to carry out aggressive patrols and ambushes but also to engage in civic action. As has frequently proven to be the case in warfare, the toughest fighting men are often far more considerate in dealing with the civilians than rear echelon types who need to show how tough they are. The All Americans proved their compassion working with the local population in many ways. Among the more noteworthy projects was a long-term one begun by the 2/321st Artillery in May 1969. Working with the local agricultural advisor, the gunners analysed the soil in their area of operations then ordered sixteen types of seeds from the USA, which they distributed along with fertilizer. The gunners continued their interest in the project after distribution, showing the locals how to plant the seeds and even running a 'state fair' type competition for the best produce.

The 3rd Brigade of the 82nd Airborne Division arrives in the Republic of Vietnam in February 1968. (*USAF*)

The 58th Signal Company laid telephone wires between local hamlets allowing them to communicate and thus enhancing their security from VC attack. In another move to enhance hamlet security, Company C, 307th Engineers assisted with the 'Hamlet Barrier Program' building berms and other protection for the villagers. Other members of the 82nd helped to train local militiamen to defend the hamlet. Individual paratroopers frequently 'adopted' local families, especially the children, and undertook such projects as trips to Saigon to visit the zoo with the children of different villages. This not only had the effect of giving the children an outing away from the war but showed them first-hand that Saigon had not been destroyed during the Tet Offensive, a claim constantly made by the VC to the rural peasants. Other All Americans paid for a Vietnamese girl to attend college in the USA to receive training as a teacher.

Civic action could only work, however, if the paratroopers ensured the security of their area of operations and of Saigon. Therefore, Brig Gen Dickerson deployed his three parachute infantry battalions in key blocking positions along the enemy infiltration and supply routes. A combination of aggressive patrols, night ambushes and cordon and search operations proved highly successful in denying the enemy access to his infiltration routes and to the hamlets which had formerly been under VC control.

Another high priority for the All Americans was the prevention of rocket attacks on Saigon proper and, especially Tan Son Nhut. Radar and other intruder detection devices—many of them developed for use on the proposed 'McNamara Line' blocking access from North Vietnam and later used along the Ho Chi Minh Trail and around Khe Sanh – were emplaced, thus allowing the paratroopers to monitor enemy movement with a minimal amount of manpower assigned. Once movement was spotted, either ambush teams could be vectored to hit the infiltrators or artillery fire or gunships could be called in to deal with them. The gunships were especially effective when operating with 'Firefly' choppers which carried high-intensity lights to illuminate the enemy and fix him like an insect for the gunship to swat.

When the enemy did fire rockets, counter fire was immediately directed at the launch sites, thus forcing the enemy to rush his volleys. To discover the potential rocket sites, saturation patrols blanketed the area, using mine detectors to unearth 107mm and 122mm rockets which had been buried near the sites preparatory to firing. So effective were the 82nd's countermeasures that, during the year they operated around Saigon, not

Members of the 82nd Airborne Division fire the .45 caliber pistol Model 1911A1 during training. (*US Army*)

A member of the 82nd Airborne Division with a barrel of phougas (field expedient napalm) used around the perimeters of fire bases and other installations to impede surprise attacks in the Republic of Vietnam. (*US Army*)

a single rocket was fired into the city from their area of operations, though they did take some fire themselves from enemy rocketeers.

The combat effectiveness of the 82nd was so high that battalions were frequently detached to take part in important operations. On 11 January 1969, for example, the 2/505th and Battery B, 2/321st Artillery joined the 1st Cavalry Division (Airmobile) for operations at Fire Support Base Eleanor, north of Phuoc Vinh. This area was still in III Corps, but in the northern part. On 17 January, elements of the 2/505th met heavy enemy resistance, engaging in a heated firefight until airstrikes and artillery forced the enemy to withdraw. Continuing their operations, the 2/505th captured a recently abandoned enemy hospital complex on 21 January. On 8 February, the 1/505th replaced the 2/505th and completed the operation, which lasted until 15 February, eventually resulting in sixty-eight enemy KIA.

A little over a month later, on 17 March, the 1/505th and Battery A, 2/321st Artillery were assigned to the 2nd Brigade, 25th Infantry, for operations west of Saigon near the Cambodian border. Due to their skill at ambush and small unit combat, the 1/505th drew the mission of interdicting infiltration routes from Cambodia towards the capital. The heavy jungle and the numerous booby traps made this area of operations particularly difficult,

Award ceremonies in the Republic of Vietnam as members of the 58th Signal Company prepare for the unit's deactivation prior to the 3rd Brigade of the 82nd returning to the USA. (*US Army*)

but the All Americans took it in their stride, albeit careful stride because of the booby traps. Heavy contact with the enemy began on 21 March and continued sporadically for the next six weeks during which the battalion inflicted ninety-two KIA on the VC/NVA and captured twenty-six.

On 2 May, the 1/508th was assigned to the 2nd Brigade, 25th Infantry, for operations north of Trang Bang where they came up against company-strength NVA regulars. On 3 May, the paratroopers were already in contact with the enemy in a tunnel/bunker complex. Artillery and airstrikes were called in, resulting in at least twenty dead VC. These operations continued for another three weeks until 24 May, the 1/508th accounting for 186 VC and NVA killed during the period. Many paratroopers being small of stature, though no less tough than their larger comrades, there was no shortage of good 'tunnel rats' to go into the enemy's underground warrens and ferret him out with tear gas and .45 automatic pistols.

By late May and early June, ARVN airborne and Ranger personnel were patroling and running ambushes along with the All Americans in preparation for taking over responsibility for the area, which they eventually did on 15 October 1969. So successful had the 3rd Brigade been in protecting Saigon that they were rewarded with the 'privilege' of expanding their

82nd Airborne flamethrower operator 'sanitizes' a hooch in the Republic of Vietnam (*US Army*)

Brig Gen George W. Dickerson, who commanded the 3rd Brigade of the 82nd Airborne in Vietnam, being presented with the Air Medal and DFC in December 1969. (*US Army*)

area of operations to the south into an area called the 'Pineapple' because of a pineapple plantation in the area. The terrain was especially tough to patrol and was filled with booby traps. However, with the help of turned Viet Cong—'Kit Carson Scouts'—the paratroopers of the 82nd soon learned to be expert at spotting booby traps. They were especially aided by the dogs and handlers of the 37th Infantry Platoon (Scout Dog), which had joined the Brigade on 29 January 1969. At night, the 'Pineapple' was covered by radar and ambush teams, once again denying the enemy a former safe area.

With their area of operations well secured, battalions continued to be used for other operations. On 2 June, the 2/505th along with ARVN forces assaulted the An Son, located east of the Saigon River and north of Hoc Mon Canal. While the Viets sealed the northern portion of the area, 2/505th strike elements were airlifted into position to sweep the area. They quickly discovered an NVA base camp, forcing the enemy to flee south where they ran into Company B, 2/505th which sprang the jaws of their trap killing twelve and capturing four. The sweep continued the next day, killing more NVA or driving them into the guns of the waiting ARVNs.

By September 1969, the 3rd Brigade had turned most of the responsibility for the area around Saigon over to the ARVNs. On 17 September, in fact,

Maj Gen John R. Deane, who commanded the 82nd Airborne Division from October 1968, to July 1970. Note that he wears his parachute wings (which bear a combat jump star) on 82nd oval and that he wears Vietnamese parachute wings on his right breast. (*US Army*)

the brigade was notified it would be deployed back to CONUS by the end of the year. However, there was still time for a final operation, a tough one at that. The All Americans took part in YORKTOWN VICTOR in southern Phu Hoa and the 'Iron Triangle.' In preparation, the 1/505th established firebase 'All American II' overlooking the 'Iron Triangle'. The flag flying over 'All American II' had flown over the White House and had been sent to the paratroopers by a Congressman who felt 'America's Honorguard' deserved the most prestigious Stars and Stripes available.

On 12 September, infantry companies of the 1/505th were inserted into the 'Iron Triangle' where the VC/NVA had been operating with impunity for some time. The arrival of the paratroopers marked the end of the enemy's freedom of movement there, as the 1/505th began to punish the enemy severely. On 16 September, the 1/505th, the US 1st Infantry and the ARVNs carried out a cordon and search of the village of Phu Hoa Dong, which accounted for twenty-nine enemy killed and seventeen captured, and the uncovering of a large cache of enemy weapons.

Throughout the remainder of September and on into October, the paratroopers carried out aggressive patroling and continued to run ambushes. They were especially successful at uncovering enemy tunnels which festooned the 'Iron Triangle.' Many contained important enemy arms or supply caches. All told the 1/505th accounted for thirty-one enemy KIA and uncovered fifty-nine separate tunnels and

124 bunkers. Needless to say, 1/505th tunnel rats were busy during YORKTOWN VICTOR.

Just south of the 'Iron Triangle,' the 1/508th was also taking part in YORKTOWN VICTOR. Moving into the area on 1 October the 1/508th carried out combined operations with the ARVNs. Like their comrades in the 1/505th, the paratroopers of the 1/508th carried out ambushes, cordon and search operations, intelligence gathering missions, and discovered tunnels – 135 of them to be exact. Various arms caches were discovered in the process and forty-one enemy were killed. B Company, 1/508th drew the assignment of defending the critical Phu Cuong bridge during YORKTOWN VICTOR, a mission which their forerunners at Normandy and in Holland could have well appreciated.

Beginning on 15 October, one battalion and its attached artillery battery stood down each fifteen days in preparation for the deployment of the 3rd Brigade, 82nd Airborne, back to the USA. Virtually all of the brigade's equipment was to be left in Vietnam and was turned in during the wind-down phase. On 11 December 1969, the 3rd Brigade, 82nd Airborne, returned to Fort Bragg to rejoin the rest of the division. A few days later, the 4th Brigade, which had been activated to bring the division to strength while the 3rd Brigade was serving in Vietnam, was de-activated.

Although the paratroopers of the 3rd Brigade serving in Vietnam had felt the frustrations that are inherent in a counter-insurgency war, they had performed very well. Unlike many conscripts sent to the Republic of Vietnam against their will, the men of the 82nd Airborne were volunteers (though some had entered the Army as draftees) with a high standard of professionalism. The 82nd Airborne Division would continue to serve as the United States' primary rapid intervention unit in the post-Vietnam era. The period of almost two years in Vietnam gave the division a chance to 'blood' its NCOs and junior officers and give them the combat experience necessary to enable them to pass on 'real-world' experience in a shooting war to the young recruits who would join the division in the future. Other Vietnam combat veterans of the 173rd Airborne Brigade, 101st Airborne Division, and 1st Cavalry (Airmobile) would also join the All Americans to make the division even more combat ready. The 82nd had always stressed realistic training, but even the most realistic training could not match night ambushes in the 'Pineapple' or the 'Iron Triangle' for teaching the basics of combat survival. Vietnam was an unpopular and frustrating conflict, but it was the only war the All Americans had, so they carried out their missions effectively there and honed their fighting skills for future conflicts. Though their combat experiences were much different from those of their forerunners who had jumped into Sicily, Normandy, or Holland, All American Vietnam vets are justifiably proud of their record and can frequently be heard answering stories of jumping into hot DZs from World War Two vets with stories of air assaulting into hot LZs!

12 OPERATION 'URGENT FURY'

On 25 October 1983, two members of the 82nd Airborne Division took part in the first US combat parachute jump since the Vietnam War and the first since World War Two by the All Americans. Operation URGENT FURY, the airborne amphibious invasion of the Caribbean island of Grenada, was launched at the request of six other tiny Caribbean states. The arrest and assassination of the Prime Minister of Grenada, Maurice Bishop, and that of many of his followers was followed by disorder on the island. Concerned by the implications, on 23 October 1983, Dominica, St Lucia, St Vincent, Montserrat, St Kitts-Nevis and Antigua of the Organization of Eastern Caribbean States (OECS), requested their larger neighbors Jamaica and Barbados as well as the United States to intervene militarily to restore stability to the region. The likelihood of a Soviet/Cuban takeover of the island, thus creating a launching pad for revolution throughout the area and terrorism against the United States and Latin America, had already caused the United States to monitor events on Grenada very carefully. The presence of about a thousand American citizens, primarily medical students and faculty, who could become hostages to a hostile government or victims of the civil war, had been occupying the National Security Council as well.

US armed forces had, in fact, received an initial alert on 19 October for a possible rescue operation to remove Americans on the strife-plagued island. Initially, Task Force 124—built around the USS *Guam*, and including the 22nd MAU (Marine Amphibious Unit), and the USS *Independence* carrier battle group, – both of which were en route to the Mediterranean—was considered sufficient for the task because the Navy and Marines were well-experienced in such operations. Therefore, on 21 October, these forces were ordered to head towards Grenada. However, as the presence of the People's Revolutionary Army (the Grenadan Armed Forces) and a substantial number of Cubans was taken into account, on the evening of 21 October, certain other units were alerted as well. These units included the 75th Rangers, 82nd Airborne, Special Forces Operational Detachment Delta, Naval SEAL Teams and the USAF 1st Special Operations Wing. Since the 82nd Airborne is constantly maintained in readiness for rapid deployment and undergoes practice alerts routinely, preparations at Fort Bragg proceeded efficiently for a possible mission. The Division Ready Force (DRF) at the time was based on the 2/325th and the DRB (Division Ready Brigade) was the 2nd Brigade.

Although the President had already been considering a lightning strike to rescue the Americans on Grenada, the request for assistance from the OECS gave US military intervention greater political acceptability. Hence, the decision was taken to launch an invasion for the purpose of restoring

Members of the 82nd Airborne land using the MC1-B-1 steerable parachute during an exercise in 1979. (*US Army*)

order and protecting American lives; the fact that Cuban and Soviet plans for the island would be thwarted as well was certainly considered another important, though less obviously stated element in the decision to intervene.

The decision taken, on the evening of 24 October, Rangers of the 1/75th and 2/75th Infantry (Ranger) and the ready forces at Fort Bragg began drawing ammunition and preparing their equipment for the invasion. Meanwhile, aboard their ships, the Marines of the 22nd MAU were preparing for an amphibious assault.

The first US troops ashore were US Navy SEALs and members of the Delta anti-terrorist unit who were parachuted in on the night of 23/24 October. They were reportedly from SEAL Team 6, the special anti-terrorist SEAL element, and were assigned the mission of occupying Government House and defending Sir Paul Scoon, the British Governor-General, until relieved.

Other SEALs landed from the sea on the night of 24/25 October to recce possible landing beaches, finding most of them poorly suited for the landing of troops and equipment, and also noting the presence of troops defending the beaches and airport. SEALs also carried out a raid to shut down Radio Free Grenada.

At 05.20 hours on the morning of 25 October, four hundred Marines from

In April 1981, members of the 82nd Airborne who have just completed a jump gather up their parachutes. (*US Army*)

22 MAU carried out a helicopter assault to seize Pearls Airport. Although they took some anti-aircraft fire, which was suppressed by Marine Cobra gunships, by 06.30 hours, the Marines had secured all of their objectives.

Less than an hour later, the Rangers arrived over Point Salines airstrip where they found themselves taking heavy ground fire. USAF AC-130 'Spectre' gunships, however, hit the anti-aircraft positions with 20mm and 40mm cannon fire, causing the gunners to abandon their weapons rapidly. Intelligence assessments of the anti-aircraft installations indicated that they would not be able to depress their weapons to fire at aircraft under 600ft (150m); therefore, the Rangers chose to jump from only 500ft (150m). Carrying maximum combat load, about five hundred Rangers shotgunned from both sides of the aircraft at about 06.00 hours. Air Force CCTs (Combat Control Team members) also jumped to act as ground controlers for the transports which would follow the Rangers once the airstrip had been secured. Initially, in fact, it had been intended that only one Ranger company would jump to secure the airstrip while the remainder of the force would be airlanding. The presence of heavy equipment and obstacles on the runway, however, necessitated a jump by all of the Rangers. Two members of the 82nd Airborne also jumped with the Rangers, including one trooper chosen for his skill at driving a bulldozer.

During the 1980 'Bright Star' exercise in Egypt an 82nd Airborne officer and his Egyptian counterpart discuss plans for a joint parachute jump. (*US Army*)

He was, in fact, making his first jump after completing jump school—in airborne slang, he was 'getting his cherry' on a combat jump.

Soon after landing, the Rangers began clearing the airstrip, the 82nd Airborne heavy equipment driver earning his CIB (Combat Infantryman's Badge) and Combat Jump Star by helping the Rangers move the equipment parked on the runway. By 06.30 hours, the runway had been cleared, and the tough Rangers of the 1/75th had hit the east flank of the Cuban positions near the airfield by 07.00 hours. As they had left their planes about an hour earlier, the Rangers of the 2/75th had been admonished by their CO, LTC Ralph Hagler: 'Rangers, be hard!' This could be considered roughly equivalent to telling a cat to 'meow' since hardness is part of being a Ranger; the Cubans were about to find out how hard! The Ranger snipers did an excellent job with their M21 snipers' rifles eliminating Cuban mortarmen, thus discouraging enemy fire support. In addition to seizing the camp, the 1/75th drove the Cubans from their beach defenses.

The 2/75th saw their share of action, too, getting their chance to 'Be Hard' when hit by a Cuban counterattack, spearheaded by three BTR-60 APCs. A combination of recoilless rifle, LAW and 'Spectre' fire soon knocked out the APCs, however, turning most of the crew members into 'Good Cubans.' Point Salines was thus secured, though sporadic sniper

Members of the 82nd Airborne turning in their parachutes after a practice jump in April 1981. (*US Army*)

Gen Roscoe Robinson Jr., who as a Major General was the first black commander of the 82nd Airborne Division from October 1976, to December 1978. (*US Army*)

fire continued to harass incoming aircraft, and the airlift of the 82nd to the island began. The first elements of the 82nd, which had taken off just after 10.00 hours, had rigged for a possible parachute assault but about two hours out from Pope AFB, they had been informed that they would be airlanding instead since the Rangers had secured the airfield.

Beginning at 14.05 hours, the first transports carrying the All Americans touched down at Point Salines and, under intermittent snipers'fire, debarked the division commanding officer, Maj Gen Edward L. Trubbough, his forward command post and a rifle company of the 2/325th. Within the next four hours the remainder of the 2/325th Airborne Infantry had landed, reinforcing the Rangers and taking over the perimeter security for the airstrip and responsibility for the captured Cubans and PRA members. The Rangers were thus freed to move out towards the True Blue medical campus to rescue the students there. As the 82nd consolidated its hold on the airfield, Cubans and PRA gathered north of the airfield. The US troop buildup was now inexorable, however, as transports followed each other in to deliver the HQ of the 82nd's 2nd Brigade and six M102 105mm Howitzers to give artillery support. These howitzers would later go into action against Cuban and PRA mortar positions in the hills around the airstrip. On the night of 25 October, as the paratroopers and Rangers dug in for

Members of the 82nd Airborne prepare for a jump with the Egyptians during 'Bright Star' exercises. The beret flash on the trooper checking his comrade's parachute is of the 504th Airborne Infantry Regiment. (*US Army*)

a night in the rain, LTC Hagler delivered another of his succinct martial bon mots when asked about the hardship his Rangers were undergoing by having to sleep in the rain: 'I never saw a rusty Ranger.'

At 07.00 hours on 26 October, the Marines finally relieved the SEALs who had protected Sir Paul Scoon at Government House throughout the first day and night of the invasion. Although they had been facing superior numbers and firepower, the twenty-two highly trained SEALs, with substantial help from AC-130 'spectre' gunships, had held out against heavy and repeated enemy attacks, sustaining a number of casualties in the process. The same day, the remainder of the American students, those on the grand Anse Campus, were rescued by Marines and Rangers.

Enemy resistance having proved more tenacious than anticipated, additional elements of the 82nd Airborne poured onto the island. The 1/505th arrived on the 26 October along with UH-60 Black Hawk helicopters of the 82nd's Combat Aviation Battalion. The Black Hawks were to receive their baptism of fire on Grenada, the Army's new troop transport carrying infantrymen into combat for the first time. With enough All Americans

82nd Airborne helicopters fly over the desert during 'Bright Star' exercises. (*US Army*)

US basic parachutist wing and pathfinder brevet.

now on the island to guard the airstrip and prisoners as well as launch an attack, paratroopers struck east from the airfield against a group of warehouses occupied by Cuban holdouts. Killing sixteen Cubans and capturing eighty-six, the troopers of the 82nd took the warehouses which contained massive stockpiles of arms and ammunition. Far more weapons than were likely to be needed by the PRA or Grenadan militia were present, including one thousand six hundred AKM assault rifles, indicating that the Cubans and Soviets did, indeed, plan to use Grenada as a base for exporting revolution and terrorism. Captured documents confirmed this fact and added even more validity to President Reagan's decision to launch URGENT FURY.

On 27 October, paratroopers of the 82nd's 2nd Brigade continued to push north, mopping up any enemy resistance encountered as they advanced. Accurate fire from the 82nd's own snipers proved a rapid and often final discouragement to holdouts sniping at the advancing All Americans. A third airborne infantry battalion of the 82nd arrived on 27 October, too, as the 1/508th was airlifted to Point Salines, granting enough reserves to deal with any likely contingency.

Troopers of the 82nd attacked the police academy on 27 October but discovered that the PRA and Cubans had abandoned their weapons and were attempting to blend with the population, though a few hardcore resisters continued to snipe at the American paratroopers. The attempt to blend with the Grenadan population by their former oppressors proved unsuccessful, however, as the Grenadans, who had welcomed the Americans as liberators, gladly pointed out the former PRA members and Cubans in their midst to the paratroopers. The Grenadans were especially impressed

Members of the 82nd Airborne Division move out on patrol after arriving on Grenada during 'Operation Urgent Fury'. Note the vest for 40mm grenades worn by the grenadier at the rear. Note also the new 'Fritz' helmets. (*Dept. of Defense*)

82nd Airborne officers wearing the desert camouflage pattern and sand colored helmet covers prepare to make a training jump in Egypt during 'Bright Star' exercises. (*US Army*)

105mm howitzers of the 82nd Airborne in action against Cuban positions during the invasion of Grenada. (*Dept. of Defense*)

to notice black officers and NCOs commanding white members of the 82nd, thus debunking the Cuban propaganda about the terrible plight of blacks in America. Beyond a doubt, the sight of a tough 82nd Airborne, Ranger or Marine black sergeant questioning the parentage and intellectual level of a white private offered graphic proof of the fallaciousness of the Cubans' assertions.

Unfortunately, on 27 October, sixteen members of the 82nd Airborne, including one who later died, were injured during a 'friendly' airstrike on Frequente. Calivigny Camp was expected to be the center of heavy resistance, so a group of Rangers airlifted by eight 82nd Aviation Battalion UH-60s was assigned to assault the camp. As it turned out, resistance was lighter than expected and the installation was secured within fifteen minutes; however, six of the Blackhawks were damaged or destroyed in the process. For the most part, this operation ended enemy resistance, though there remained a few holdouts in the hills. Over the next few days, the troopers of the 82nd linked up with the Marines at St George's and continued to patrol and search for any PRA or Cubans remaining

Members of the 82nd Airborne learning to live in the desert during Operation 'Bright Star'. (*US Army*)

at large. The 82nd net caught a big fish when they captured General Austin who had headed the Grenadan armed forces and who had helped depose and murder Maurice Bishop. On 2 November, the 82nd, along with the Caribbean Peacekeeping Force, took over responsibility for security on the island from the Rangers and Marines who had been redeployed. One very 'rewarding' task for the 82nd was supervising the 'evacuation' of over one hundred diplomats from Communist Bloc or Communist Bloc-allied countries, such as Libya, at the request of Sir Paul Scoon.

Although the military operation had ended by early November, elements of the 82nd Airborne would remain to help to provide security and help the islanders repair the damage caused by the invasion. At one point, approximately six thousand members of the 82nd Airborne had been committed to the Grenadan operation, though not all had deployed to the island; most of those who had gone returned to Fort Bragg relatively rapidly. URGENT FURY had offered a chance to test the division's ability to deploy rapidly when needed. The first aircraft carrying troopers of the 82nd Airborne had touched down at Point Salines only seventeen hours after notification that the operation was to be launched.

On a more individual level, junior officers and NCOs got a chance to test their training under fire, thus hardening them for any future operational deployments and giving them valuable live-fire experience. The fact that the Rangers, Marines and 82nd Airborne paratroopers were actually sent on a combat deployment will also lend immediacy to training in the future, helping to keep the edge needed by troops earmarked for such missions and forced to train constantly to maintain readiness. Grenada also helped to dispel the negative view of the US armed forces left over by the Vietnam War. The black beret of the Rangers and the maroon beret of the 82nd Airborne have been worn with a bit more pride since the Grenada operation.

Certain new concepts and equipment received their final 'field testing' on Grenada. The Kevlar 'Fritz' helmet worn by the 82nd Airborne troopers, for example, saved at least a couple of paratroopers' lives, thus immensely increasing the confidence in its viability of their comrades also wearing the new 'plastic pot', not to mention keeping alive a couple of highly trained soldiers. The broadened array of military specializations open to women soldiers also received a test on Grenada as four female Airborne MPs of the XVIIIth Airborne Corps' 16th MP Brigade were deployed to guard prisoners and perform security duties on the island.

Though URGENT FURY was certainly not an operation with the combat intensity of such World War Two 82nd commitments as MARKET GARDEN, nor did it involve such sustained combat as Vietnam, it still showed that the All Americans can perform their essential mission by deploying rapidly and going into combat. The Cubans and Soviets were also sent a very clear message about expansionism in the Western Hemisphere, a message ably delivered by the Rangers, Marines and 82nd Airborne!

13 EIGHTEEN HOURS TO WHEELS UP

Today's 82nd Airborne Division – wielding more firepower than all seven Allied airborne divisions of World War Two combined – has the mission of deploying anywhere in the world with little or no prior notice, going immediately into combat upon arrival, and winning! Twenty-four hours a day, seven days a week, fifty-two weeks a year, a contingent of the All Americans remains on alert ready to begin deployment into battle. This deployment might well mean jumping without secured airfields to seize an airhead or beachhead through which the divisional buildup can continue, to be followed by the arrival of the heavier armored infantry or armored divisions which might be committed in the wake of the paratroopers.

Although the 82nd Airborne Division can be delivered to battle via parachute or helicopter, troopers remain infantrymen who must cover a lot of ground on foot as this trooper certainly realizes. (*US Army*)

82nd Airborne TOW team gives portable yet formidable anti-tank capability to the division. (*82nd Airborne*)

Member of the 82nd Airborne wearing the 'Fritz' helmet emplaces a Claymore Mine. (*Harris Pubs*)

Within eighteen hours of the 'Go!' order, the 82nd is expected to be wheels up and on its way to act as the 'point unit' for the entire US Army. This is a highly critical mission which requires flexibility and preparedness by every member of the 82nd Airborne from the commanding general to the company cook, all of whom are parachute qualified. In fact, during a total divisional commitment virtually one hundred per cent of the division would be expected to chute up, board their transport aircraft at Pope Air Force Base and jump into combat anywhere in the world.

To allow the most rapid possible commitment of the 82nd to combat and to allow flexible response to missions requiring varying levels of fighting power, the 82nd's rapid deployment strategy is based on an incremental or 'building block' system. Four blocks of increasing size act as the steps for divisional commitment.

The most basic of the increments is the Initial Ready Company (IRC), which consists of an airborne infantry company augmented by an artillery forward observer team, totalling about one hundred and eighty-five men. The IRC has all of its equipment pre-rigged for parachute drop and is able to emplane and go 'wheels up' almost immediately if necessary. It is the IRC which would be the first to jump with the mission of scouting and securing the DZs for the follow-up increments of the division.

First to follow-up the IRC would be the Division Ready Force (DRF) which is based on one of the division's nine airborne infantry battalions augmented by an artillery battery, an engineer platoon, an MP squad, a chopper crew, etc., totalling about one thousand men. The IRC is normally drawn from the DRF.

The third increment, expected to go 'wheels up' in eighteen hours, is the Division Ready Brigade (DRB). With its approximately three thousand five hundred troops, the DRB is the primary task organization. Comprising three airborne infantry battalions, an anti-tank company and an artillery battalion of eighteen 105mm Howitzers, the DRB has an impressive amount of combat potential. For specific missions, it can be augmented with armor, air defense batteries, air cavalry or other divisional units as needed.

The final block is the entire 18,000 strong 82nd Airborne Division, which can be parachuted or air dropped in its entirety. Although exercises are run constantly to test the 82nd's rapid deployment capability, the invasion of Grenada offered the best test of all, a live-fire test the All Americans passed with honors, beating their eighteen hour target for brigade commitment substantially.

To keep the finely honed edge needed by the troopers of the 82nd Airborne, Emergency Deployment Readiness Exercises (EDREs) are run frequently. At least once a month, in fact, an EDRE is conducted without

Challenge coin carried by past and present members of the 82nd Airborne Division to prove their service with the All Americans.

Members of the 325th Infantry firing a LAW. (*US Army*)

notice. These exercises often include an off-post deployment, a three day tactical exercise, and then redeployment to Fort Bragg.

As an example of the rapidity of global response made possible by the 82nd's incremental system of commitment and constant readiness training, assume a hypothetical need for US troops in the Eastern Mediterranean. Deploying to Adana AFB, Turkey, from Fort Bragg with no prior notice aboard C-141s, the IRC would touch down within thirty-five hours, the DRF in forty-eight hours, the DRB in eighty-two hours and the division in 264 hours.

If necessary, all supplies needed by the division can be airdropped using CDS (Container Delivery System). Using this system, in one pass a C-130 can drop sixteen containers and a C-141 can drop twenty-eight each of 2,000lb (910kg). This system is very accurate and eliminates much of the scattering of supplies which has plagued airborne forces in the past. Another system which can be used during resupply is LAPES (Low Altitude Parachute Extraction System). Primarily designed for the delivery of heavy items such as the M551 Sheridan armored recon vehicle,

UH-1D helicopters of the 82nd Aviation Battalion landing troops during an air assault exercise at Fort Bragg. (*US Army*)

LAPES needs a clearing of at least 66ft (20m) wide by 490ft (150m) long. Once such a clearing is marked as the DZ, the aircraft descends to about 10ft (3m) above the ground at 150 knots and a parachute pulls the load from the aircraft. The load, which has been lashed to reinforced pallets, then slides along the ground to a stop.

A great aid to precise delivery of airborne troops, equipment and re-supply of drops is AWADS (Adverse Weather Aerial Delivery Systems), a navigation system which allows a pilot to fly precisely to a drop zone in fog, rain, haze, clouds, dark or other conditions which would normally inhibit operations. Because AWADS allows a precise supply drop or parachute assault in darkness or poor weather conditions, the element of surprise is enhanced, while many of the scattering problems inherent in World War Two parachute operations are eliminated.

These tactical improvements in delivery methods allow the 82nd Airborne Division to jump, seize, and hold a far larger airhead, against stiffer opposition, than previously possible since it is no longer necessary to defend a fixed base within the area unless it is a mission objective, such as an airfield needed for follow-up troops.

The much greater anti-aircraft and anti-tank capability of the contemporary 82nd Airborne gives far more staying power in the face of serious enemy opposition. Initial anti-aircraft capability rests with sixty-three Redeye teams, some of which jump with the lead elements and are then used to defend battalion level HQs or logistic facilities against air attack. Heavier anti-aircraft firepower is present at brigade level in the Vulcan multi-barrel 20mm gun. Each brigade has a Vulcan battery with twelve guns, plus an additional battery to defend the divisional HQ and logistics center. The Vulcan can be delivered by either air drop or LAPES and moved about the battlefield by Gamma Goat, helicopter or jeep. Though the Vulcan is an extremely effective system, it is scheduled to be replaced by the even more effective M988 40mm Sergeant York system. Should extremely heavy air opposition – for example, a large concentration of Soviet Hind gunships – be expected, XVIIIth Airborne Corps' Hawk missile batteries might be deployed as well.

Traditionally, tanks have been the bane of the paratrooper, but the troopers of the 82nd Airborne are well-equipped and well-trained to deal with enemy armor. Should armored opposition be expected, each trooper would jump with an M-72 LAW (Light Anti-Tank Weapon), with which he is trained to attack armor from the vulnerable flanks and rear, and possibly with anti-tank mines. Each battalion is additionally equipped with thirty M47 Dragon anti-tank missile systems. The M65 TOW (Tube-launched, Optically-tracked, Wire-guided) provides the division with an even more potent anti-tank missile system. Each airborne infantry battalion is equipped with twelve TOWs. Another eighteen TOWs are available with each brigade's anti-tank company. Normally, the TOW system is delivered by heavy drop, but it can be broken into six components, each jumped by an individual trooper, thus giving it great versatility. Divisional artillery or armor or airstrikes called in by USAF Combat Control Teams, which jump with the 82nd, could be used against large concentrations of enemy armor.

Just as equipment has evolved during the almost half century the 82nd Airborne has been in existence, so have tactics. The MC-1B steerable parachute, for example, allows very accurate delivery of troops. Frequently, this ability to insert individual troopers accurately is used to place anti-armor outposts on the flanks of a major drop. These outposts often include troops trained to use laser-designators to pinpoint targets for supporting aircraft to deliver 'smart' bombs or missiles. Other anti-armor weapons such as the LAW, Dragon or TOW may be incorporated in such outposts to slow and identify enemy armor before it reaches the main airborne force. Motorcycle-borne troopers of the 1/17th Cavalry may also act as anti-armor scouts.

Should heavy concentrations of enemy armor be encountered at the outposts, TOW equipped choppers (Cobras or AH-64s) can pop up and engage the armor. The division's fifty-four Sheridan light armored vehicles with their 152mm missile/gun system may be used as tank destroyers, too, launching a Shillelagh missile or using gunfire as needed. Deliverable by LAPES, heavy drop or airlanding, the Sheridan gives the 82nd mobility and firepower in a tracked vehicle weighing about 35,000lb (15,875kg) due to its aluminium hull.

After a recent reorganisation to bring the 82nd in line with the Army's regimental system, the 82nd Airborne Division's components are now as follows:

82nd Airborne Division, 1988

1st Brigade
  1/504th, 2/504th, 3/504th, Company E (Anti-Armor)/504th
    Parachute Infantry Battalions
2nd Brigade
  1/325th, 2/325th, 3/325th, Company E (Anti-Armor)/325th
    Parachute Infantry Battalions
3rd Brigade
  1/505th, 2/505th, 3/505th, Company E (Anti-Armor)/505th
  Parachute Infantry Battalions

Divisional Artillery
  1/319th, 2/319th, 3/319th Field Artillery Battalions
    Battery B/26th Target Acquisition Battery

Other Divisional Units
  1/17th Armored Cavalry Squadron
  3rd Battalion, 4th Air Defense Artillery
  4th Battalion, 68th Armor

Member of the 82nd Airborne Division prepares to fire a Redeye anti-aircraft missile. (*US Army*)

82nd Combat Aviation Battalion,
20th Aviation Battalion (AH-64 Attack Helicopters)
313th Military Intelligence Battalion
307th Engineer Battalion
82nd Signal Battalion
82nd Military Police Company
Divisional HQ and HQ Company
14th Chemical Detachment

Division Support Command (DISCOM)
782nd Maintenance Battalion
307th Medical Battalion
407th Supply and Service Battalion
82nd Administrative Company
82nd Finance Company
182nd Material and Management Center

To prepare these components for their diverse missions, today's 82nd

Trainee undergoing basic parachute training prepares to make a jump. (*US Army*)

Airborne undertakes one of the most intensive training regimens in the US armed forces. This training may take place virtually anywhere in the world and may include parachute or air assault and live-fire. Each infantry platoon, company and battalion must undergo a day and a night combined arms live-fire exercise semi-annually. Mortars and hand grenades as well as rifles are normally employed during these exercises. Frequently, anti-armor weapons, artillery and helicopters will be involved as well. During these exercises, the division annually expends over three million rounds of machine gun ammunition and over one hundred and thirty thousand rounds of mortar and artillery ammunition.

Each battalion must conduct one off-post training exercise every year, too. In addition to training all over the United States, 82nd Airborne components have trained in Korea, Egypt, Greece, Turkey, Panama, Great Britain, Spain and Italy, among other foreign countries. Frequently, such training will include a parachute jump with local airborne troops, thus allowing an exchange of skills with allied paratroopers and allowing members of the 82nd to win the right to wear foreign parachute wings on their right breast.

Normally, at any given time, an airborne infantry battalion will be on one of three training cycles. Post Support, the lightest of these cycles, entails guard duty, acting as an 'aggressor' unit or carrying out other details. Intensive Training involves continuous field training and live-fire exercises. Division Ready Force is the third cycle.

Approximately one-third of all training is at night to prepare the paratroopers of the 82nd to counter the Soviet tactic of around-the-clock combat. During some training cycles, a battalion will take part in a two-week field exercise during which they sleep in the daytime and carry out their training at night. As a unit likely to be committed to a hostile, possibly contaminated battlefield, the 82nd Airborne gets extensive NBC (Nuclear, Biological, Chemical) training. For example, annually every trooper is required to fire his rifle or crew-served weapon while wearing full NBC gear. At least some members of the division have also made training parachute jumps in full NBC suits.

MOUT (Military Training in Urban Terrain) training has assumed even greater importance as US troops have been committed to urban security duties in Beirut. Building clearing involving coordinated movements, fields of fire and the use of grenades is one of the most important skills learned during the MOUT training given the 82nd in the mock city at Fort Bragg.

Interspersed with all of the other training, the troopers of the 82nd must maintain their high state of physical fitness. A combination of running, team sports, calisthenics, hand-to-hand combat, weight training and other physical activities keeps the individual fitness level among the highest in the Army. Each trooper in the division, for example, runs an average of seven hundred miles per year. 82nd Airborne boxers, martial artists, weight lifters, football players and other competitive athletes have established themselves among the Army's toughest competitors – the combination of the paratroopers' tenacity and willingness to 'drive on' under adverse conditions merged with the division's rigorous physical training making for superb athletes.

The 82nd Airborne's packed training schedule is not, however, intended to turn out athletes, though excellent conditioning is certainly helpful in performing the division's mission. The 82nd has also won well-deserved fame for smartness, which is one reason for the unit being known as 'America's Honor Guard.' Once again, however, the precision and discipline that makes the 82nd an impressive parade ground unit are intended to create not just an Honor Guard but a vanguard capable of spearheading American military commitment to combat rapidly and effectively as the IRC, then the DRF, then the DRB, and finally the entire division inexorably answers the call to arms.

XVIIIth Airborne Corps

No consideration of the current 82nd Airborne Division would be complete without mentioning the XVIIIth Airborne Corps, of which the 82nd is a part. Currently, four divisions are assigned to the XVIIIth Airborne Corps: the 82nd Airborne, the 101st Airborne (Air Assault), the 10th Mountain Division (Light Infantry) and the 24th Infantry Division (Mechanized). Among the additional units comprising the 82nd are 1st Corps Support Command, 16th Military Police Brigade, 20th Engineer Brigade, 18th Field Artillery Brigade, 35th Signal Brigade, 194th Armor Brigade, 197th Infantry Brigade, 525th Military Intelligence Group and the 'Dragon Brigade.'

Since January 1983, the US Central Command has been charged with providing the US multi-service rapid deployment capability, with the US Army contingent coming from the XVIIIth Airborne Corps. As units of the XVIIIth are committed to operations, they may be augmented by Corps assets as the 82nd was by military police personnel on Grenada. Controlling as it does the United States' most combat ready troops, the XVIIIth Airborne Corps staff and corps components maintain a high state of fitness and readiness themselves with contingency plans for commitment to virtually all parts of the world being constantly updated.

M102 Light 105mm howitzers of the 82nd Airborne Division firing during live-fire exercises. (*US Army*)

C-130 aircraft bringing in reinforcements of the 82nd Airborne Division to the airhead seized by the Army's Rangers earlier in 'Operation Urgent Fury.'

14 THE MOST DEADLY WEAPON OF ALL

The US Paratrooper

The 82nd Airborne Division remains the USA's most combat ready division as a result of intensive and constant training. Previous chapters have discussed some of the exercises and unit training which help the 82nd to hone its razor edge, but it is the individual airborne infantryman who remains the most effective weapon in the All American arsenal and it is some of the specialized individual training he or she receives which will be discussed in this chapter.

Basic Parachute Training

The basic prerequisite for almost every member of the 82nd Airborne Division is basic parachute training—'Jump School' as it is most widely known. Conducted at the US Army Infantry Center at Fort Benning, Ga, by the 4th Airborne Training Battalion, the Basic Airborne Course lasts

Troopers undergoing basic parachute training at Fort Benning on the 34ft mock tower. (*US Army*)

82nd Airborne troopers jumping into Germany during a 'Spearpoint' exercise in Germany during 1980. (*US Army*)

three gruelling weeks. Unlike Great Britain and some other countries which have a pre-parachute course selection program, the toughening up process is incorporated into US parachute training and normally results in about ten per cent of those beginning the course failing to complete it.

Prior to acceptance for the course, students must pass a medical examination and the Army Physical Readiness Test, thus assuring some degree of preparedness for the rugged physical training incorporated into jump school. Each morning of the first two weeks begins with an hour of PT (Physical Training), including a 3 mile (4.81km) run, increased one day a week to 4 miles (6.4km). Many graduates of jump school believe that the US parachute badge should incorporate a soldier doing pushups rather than a parachute, so ubiquitous is this exercise, which is assigned for even tiny infractions during training. Ten pushups is the standard penalty, but trainees are expected always to do one more than assigned for Airborne to show their willingness to drive on just a little further. This airborne spirit extends to substituting the word 'Airborne' for 'Yes' when addressing the 'Black Hat' training NCOs; thus instead of 'Yes, sergeant' to an instruction, the reply would be 'Airborne, sergeant!'

The physical training remains only an adjunct to the school's primary mission—teaching the basics of jumping out of 'a perfectly good airplane;' therefore, between thirty-five and forty hours per week are devoted to instruction in the use of the parachute to carry the soldier into combat. Each of the course's three weeks is designated by the type of training undergone – Ground Week, Tower Week and Jump Week.

In addition to inculcating the trainee with a sense of the US airborne tradition, Ground Week teaches each trainee the basics of exiting an aircraft, donning and adjusting a parachute harness and doing PLFs (Parachute Landing Falls). The thirty-three hours of instruction during this week include two hours of airborne orientation, five hours on the mock door learning proper exiting procedures and drill within the aircraft, twelve hours on the 34ft (10.4km) mock tower gaining the confidence to step out into space, and fourteen hours practicing PLFs from the landing fall towers—with the ground seeming harder each hour. Mock door and mock tower work as well as training on the lateral drift apparatus help to teach body control when exiting the aircraft and parachute control.

The second week sees the trainees moving to the 250ft (76.2m) tower, though nine more hours are also spent on the mock door and 34ft mock tower with emphasis now on mass exits. Eleven hours are spent in guided

Troopers of the 82nd Airborne after parachuting into Germany after a direct flight across the Atlantic during a NATO reinforcement exercise in 1980. (*US Army*)

Various 82nd Airborne pocket patches (mostly unauthorized), including from top left: 82nd Signals (locally made in Vietnam), 82nd Command and Control, 325th Infantry, 2nd Brigade Recon, 505th Infantry (locally made in Vietnam), 82nd Support, Multinational Peacekeeping Force in the Sinai, and Rapid Deployment Force.

descents from the 250ft tower and another eleven hours are spent in the suspended harness (where one's more intimate portions soon inform of a poorly adjusted parachute harness) and the swing landing tower. The wind machine (similar to those used on film sets) is used in learning to recover after landings. Another very critical skill learned during tower week is the ability to deal with various types of malfunctions.

The third week sees those trainees who have successfully completed the first two weeks progress to the five static line parachute jumps which will make them US paratroopers; never again will they be a 'leg'. Of the five required jumps, two are from 1,250ft (380m), two from 1,500ft (455m) and one from 2,000ft (610m). Three are with the old standby T-10 parachute, while two are with the MC1-1B steerable parachute. Included are one night jump and two with equipment.

The five jumps completed, the new paratroopers receive their parachute wings. Traditionally, the sons or daughters of former paratroopers have their wings pinned on by their airborne parent, and today it is not unheard of to have three generations of paratroopers represented in one family. Some of the newly badged paratroopers will never make another

Basic parachute trainee making a descent from the 250 ft tower. (*US Army*)

Maj Gen James Lindsey who took command of the 82nd Airborne in February 1981. (*US Army*)

jump in their military careers, but they will retain the pride in their own accomplishment and the respect for and of others who wear the parachute wings. Others will report to units such as the 82nd Airborne to make their sixth jump – their 'cherry jump.' For those serving with airborne units, parachute jumping will become part of the job, but except for those who may make a combat jump, it is unlikely that subsequent jumps will match that first 'exit from a plane in flight' during jump week at Fort Benning.

HALO and Other Specialized Parachuting Techniques

Although mass static line jumps are the primary parachute insertion method used by the troopers of the 82nd Airborne, there are still situations in which free fall parachute insertions or other specialized jumping techniques may be called for, especially among small recon or raiding elements. As a result, a number of All Americans are qualified in such techniques.

HALO (High Altitude Low Opening) parachute training is given in a five week course at Fort Bragg, the home of the 82nd Airborne. The first skill the students must learn before mastering the art of free fall parachuting is body control prior to deploying the chute. Since the HALO jumper will be free falling with rucksack, weapon and a 50lb (23kg) parachute, stable body positioning is a must, and great stress is placed on learning the 'starfish' position with arms and legs spread while the body arches. Maneuvring, emergency deployment of the reserve chute, use of the altimeter, breathing on oxygen while jumping, and orientation about hypoxia, hyperventilation, decompression and the extreme heat and cold encountered are all learned as well during the preliminary stages of HALO training.

Once the basics are mastered, the students move on to their first free fall jumps from the beginning altitude of 12,500ft (3,810m) from which they will make eleven jumps, for many the first they will have made without a static line. Their initial free fall jumps under their harness, they progress to 17,500ft (5,335m) where they learn to jump using oxygen masks, and then finally progress to 25,000ft (7,620m) for their final jumps. During the training, at least two night jumps are made. By the end of the course, free fallers feel comfortable with falling for up to two minutes at a speed of 125mph (200km/hr) or more!

Experienced HALO jumpers are now also learning newer advanced techniques such as HAHO (High Altitude High Opening) in which a jump is made at very high altitude, such as 30,000ft (9,145m) and the airfoil chute is then opened soon after exiting the aircraft. This method allows

Troopers of the 325th Infantry prepare a 107mm mortar for firing during live-fire training during 1981. (*US Army*)

Variations of the 82nd Airborne shoulder sleeve insignia, from top left: World War II, current, locally made in Vietnam, sniper (locally made in Vietnam), pocket patch for recondo graduates, unauthorized Grenada veterans, unauthorized Grenada veterans, two baseball cap variants.

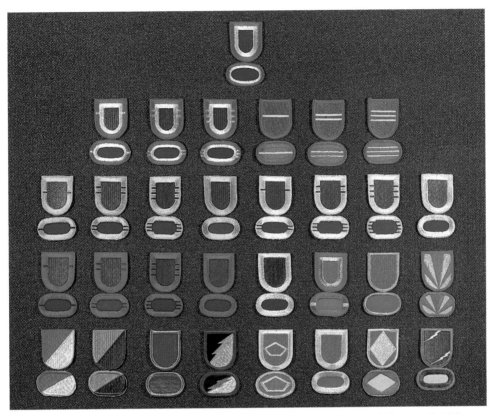

Current beret flashes and parachute ovals in wear by members of the 82nd Airborne Division: *top* 82nd Airborne Division; *2nd row, left to right* 1st Brigade, 2nd Brigade, 3rd Brigade, 1/319th Artillery, 2/319th, 3/319th; *3rd row, left to right* 1/504th, 2/504th, 3/504th, Company E (Anti-Armor)/504th, 1/325th, 2/325th, 3/325th, Company E (Anti-Armor)/325th; *4th row, left to right* 1/505th, 2/505th, 3/505th, Company E (Anti-Armor)/505th, 307th Medical Battalion, 407th Supply and Service Battalion, 782nd Maintenance Battalion, 3rd Battalion/4th Air Defense Artillery (ADA); *5th row, left to right* 1st Squadron/17th Cavalry, 4th Battalion/68th Armor, 82nd Combat Aviation Battalion, 20th Aviation Battalion, 82nd Signal Battalion, 307th Engineer Battalion, 618th Engineer Company, 313th Military Intelligence Battalion. (*Val Schweickhardt*)

a team to assemble in the air and then glide for miles into an area so far away that no one will have heard the noise of the delivery aircraft.

LAHS (Low Altitude High Speed) is another specialized method in which jumpers are extracted from the aircraft at high speed at very low altitudes, 150–200ft (45–60m).

Although all of these insertion methods are best suited for small clandestine teams such as a Special Forces Operational Detachment, they grant a limited number of members of the 82nd Airborne the capability to conduct clandestine raiding or intelligence operations at the divisional level.

Golden Knights

For those members of the 82nd Airborne who are free fall qualified, the US Army Parachute Team – the Golden Knights – offers both a challenge

82nd Airborne machine gunner during training exercises at Fort Bragg (*Harris Pubs*)

and a chance to increase their parachuting skills even more. Normally, the 82nd is well represented among the Golden Knights, generally supplying about one-third of the team's personnel. The expertise these All Americans gain often results, too, in more effective training techniques and equipment for the division.

The Golden Knights consist of eighty members, including six women, some of them outstanding jumpers. The two thirteen-person demonstration teams – designated the Black and the Gold Teams – give about one hundred and fifty demonstrations each per year and are the most visible portion of the Golden Knights. Other members of the team represent the US Army nationally and internationally in parachute competitions. The competitive teams are divided into a seven-member style and accuracy team and a ten-member relative work team.

Complementing their demonstration and competition missions is the Golden Knights' third mission: testing new parachuting equipment and techniques prior to incorporating them into the regular airborne units such as the 82nd Airborne, Special Forces or Rangers. Although the Golden Knights are based at Fort Bragg, the team members are on the road much of the year as they make between twenty thousand and twenty-five thousand jumps annually.

Member of the 82nd Airborne Division, his helmet camouflaged and M-16 at the ready during training exercises at Fort Bragg. (*Harris Pubs*)

Applicants for the Golden Knights must have at least one hundred and fifty free fall jumps. From those meeting this requirement, the top applicants are put through a six-week tryout program and then, if selected, have to maintain a high rate of proficiency. Although the Golden Knights perform a very valuable service to the paratroopers of the 82nd Airborne by testing new equipment and concepts, perhaps their greatest value lies in the pride they give the individual paratrooper in being an American and especially in being an American paratrooper.

Air Assault School

Although the 82nd is an airborne division, air mobility via the division's helicopters remains another important vertical envelopment option. The ability to insert troopers via helicopter or parachute offers far greater tactical flexibility than the division possessed when the parachute or glider were its only methods of insertion onto the battlefield.

As a result, one of the most important specialized training schools attended by members of the All Americans is the Air Assault School at Fort Campbell, KY, the home of their old rivals and comrades of the 101st Air Assault Division.

Radioman of the 82nd Airborne prior to moving out after a parachute landing. (*82nd Airborne*)

Paratroopers of the 82nd Airborne Division exit the rear of a C-130 during a training jump. (*USAF*)

Any paratroopers who might come into the rugged ten day Air Assault Course believing it will be easy by comparison to jump school soon change their minds, especially since the instructors, primarily from the 101st Airborne, take great pleasure in helping to alter their view of air assault. Many traditions and 'teaching methods' of the Air Assault School are, in fact, similar to those used at jump school. Pushups, for example, are a favourite of the air assault instructors, too, with their own special variation, of course. In addition to the standard ten pushups for mistakes, the air assault instructors may assign 'pushups to the four winds' in which the trainee must drop for ten and then turn 90 degrees for ten more until all four directions have received their share. Additional physical training includes exercises, runs and hand-to-hand combat training. Especially dreaded is physical training in groups of eight with the 400lb log.

As with jump school, the physical training is only the ketchup on the C-rations, though, as the course is primarily designed to teach the student the methods of going into or out of battle via helicopter. During Phase I of the Air Assault course, the trainee learns medical extraction via helicopter, combat air assault techniques, general helicopter familiarization and pathfinder skills, including hand signals for bringing helicopters into LZs (Landing Zones) as well as marking LZs.

Phase II instructs the trainee in rappeling skills and insertion via rope or trooper ladder from a helicopter. Initially, the trainee learns to rig a swiss seat and to rappel down the 35ft (10.7m) tower. The face forward Australian rappel is always one of the more 'interesting' aspects of rappel training. Troopers from the 82nd learn to grit their teeth and drive on when the instructors tell them they have to wave at the boldly painted 101st Air Assault eagle before beginning to rappel. Once the basic skills are mastered, the trainees move on to complete six rappels from a helicopter at 90ft (27.5m).

The final phase – Phase III – teaches such skills as sling loading and rigging and wraps up the course with a 10 mile (16km) road march in full gear. Those students successfully completing the course receive their Air Assault badge, which in the case of the troopers of the 82nd Airborne, joins their parachute wings on their left breast.

Ranger and Recondo

The US Ranger course is considered one of the toughest and most effective elite light infantry courses in the world. Although a large number of Ranger trained soldiers are needed for the three Ranger battalions and the light infantry divisions, the 82nd Airborne has traditionally had a substantial number of men who wear the Ranger tab with pride. Regular Army officers and senior NCOs assigned to the 82nd particularly include a large number of Rangers since the Ranger skills are of special applicability to the 82nd's mission of deploying and fighting anywhere in the world.

The Ranger course begins at Fort Benning, with later phases conducted

Maj Gen Thomas Tackaberry who commanded the 82nd Airborne from October 1974 to October 1976. Note the Ranger tab on his left shoulder and his 'Master Blaster' parachute wings. (*US Army*)

at other venues. Normally fifty-eight days long, the course was lengthened in 1986 to sixty-five days better to accommodate the desert training phase added a few years ago to prepare American fighting men for a possible conflict in the Middle East.

During the almost continuous training, which includes nearly one thousand one hundred hours in the fifty-eight day course, approximately fifty per cent of it at night, the Ranger learns to deal with inadequate food or sleep and extreme physical and mental strain; he learns that he can push himself much further than he had ever realized he could and thus accomplish extremely difficult missions. The Ranger not only comes out of the course with a greater depth of knowledge about making war but with a greater knowledge about himself.

During the eighteen day initial phase of training at Fort Benning, Ranger trainees are frequently up at 02.30 hours and taking part in rugged physical training by 03.30 hours. Ranger trainees double time everywhere and are constantly assigned pushups for mistakes. By the end of the Benning phase, runs will be of 5 miles (8km) in length. Hand-to-hand combat and the use of the knife or bayonet are important parts of physical training and take on their own ambience at 03.30 hours in the morning. Other skills enhanced during the Benning phase include map reading and land navigation, demolitions, calling in artillery fire support, reconnaissance (including the use of night vision devices) and combat patroling. At the end of the phase, an examination over forty-three tasks must be passed.

The next phase is the mountain phase at Dahlonoga, GA, where the trainees spend seventeen days learning military mountaineering skills such as rappeling, rock climbing and building rope bridges. The 'High Point' of this phase is a night 200ft (60m) rappel. Patroling – emphasized throughout Ranger training – is practiced in rough terrain as are recon operations during this phase.

The trainees next parachute into Fort Bliss, TX, for a week of desert training. Working up to twenty-two hours a day, they learn desert survival and patroling, practice airborne and air landing operations and take part in a live-fire simulated raid.

The eighteen-day Florida phase begins with another parachute insertion. (Trainees make up to six jumps during Ranger training, an added bonus for the 82nd's paratroopers undergoing the course.) Small boat operations, stream crossing, platoon operations in swamps and jungles, counter guerrilla operations (against tough Ranger 'aggressors'), and SERE (Survival, Escape, Resistance, Evasion) training—these combine to make the Florida phase the toughest of all. Averaging up to twenty-one hours per day and coming after a month-and-a-half of previous training, the Florida phase brings Ranger training to its grueling end.

Those awarded the Ranger tab for successful completion of the course wear it with justifiable pride and return to their units as more effective soldiers.

The XVIIIth Airborne Corps runs it own mini-Ranger course known as the Recondo course. Drawing its title from the combination of the words 'Reconnaissance' and 'Commando,' this two-week course covers military mountaineering, wilderness survival, combat first aid, land navigation, stream crossing, immediate action drills, helicopter rappeling and other skills associated with the Ranger course, though not with the same depth or intensity. Recondo graduates offer an excellent complement to the Ranger trained personnel and allow a much larger portion of the 82nd's enlisted personnel to receive training in valuable skills.

Current Distinctive Insignia (DIs) worn on the beret flashes by members of the 82nd Airborne Division: *top row, left to right* 82nd Airborne Division, 504th Infantry, 325th Infantry; *2nd row, left to right* 505th Infantry, 319th Artillery, 307th Medical Battalion; *3rd row, left to right* 407th Supply and Service Battalion, 782nd Maintenance Battalion, 3rd Battalion/4th Air Defense Artillery; *4th row, left to right* 1st Squadron/17th Cavalry, 4th Battalion/68th Armor, 82nd Combat Aviation Battalion; *5th row, left to right* 82nd Signal Battalion, 307th Engineer Battalion, 313th Military Intelligence Battalion. (*Val Schweickhardt*)

Jungle Warfare Training

As America's primary strategic reserve, the 82nd Airborne Division must be ready to fight in desert, jungle or arctic wastes. As a result, specialized training for combat in these environments is an important part of the division's readiness. One primary source of such specialized environmental training for the All Americans is the JOTC (Jungle Operations Training Center) located at Fort Sherman in the Panama Canal Zone. The course, which lasts for three weeks, is given for company or battalion sized units, and elements of the 82nd Airborne are frequent attendees, as can be attested by the number of 'Jungle Expert' pocket patches one can see proudly worn at Fort Bragg.

The basic JOTC course instructs in certain standard skills such as jungle living, hygiene and survival, land navigation, communications in the jungle (including the rigging of antennas amidst heavy jungle canopy), waterborne operations, jungle close quarters battle and patroling and a tough obstacle course. Unit commanding officers select additional specialized skill areas which they feel would be especially beneficial to their troopers. Among these additional training areas frequently selected for soldiers of the 82nd are booby traps, demolitions, airmobile insertions and extractions, mortar exercises, ambush, raids, C-130 re-supply, vertical extraction, reconnaissance, helocasting and scout swimming.

One of the real benefits of the JOTC course is that it not only improves the individual trooper's skills and confidence in his ability to fight and survive in a hostile environment—to discover for himself that the jungle really is neutral—but it also builds esprit de corps within the company or battalion as all unit members have the shared experience of having undergone hardships together.

Sniper

The sniper has proven one of the most cost-effective weapons on the battlefield throughout the history of rifled arms and even earlier in the persons of skilled slingers, longbowmen and crossbowmen. Among the paratroopers of the 82nd Airborne Division, the sniper is especially valued since the division is likely to be involved in low intensity conflicts where the selective deadliness of the sniper can prove invaluable. In the Dominican Republic, Vietnam and Grenada, All American snipers proved their worth many times over. As a result, expert marksmen from the division continue to be sent to the XVIIIth Airborne Corps Advanced Marksmanship Training Unit (AMTU) for instruction.

Living up to their motto of 'One shot, One Kill,' the AMTU's five-week course is considered one of the most valuable training courses in the Army and produces snipers expert in both fieldcraft and marksmanship. Using the M21 sniper system, the troopers learn to deliver long range precision fire in support of combat operations. To allow them to perform their mission, however, they must also become experts at infiltration, building 'hides', and watching for and identifying their target.

Each class consists of about thirty troopers already expert on the M-16 rifle. They begin by learning how snipers are employed during the advance, attack, defense and retreat. Intensive training in land navigation, observation, target selection and identification, range estimation, camouflage, selection of a hide, use of various types of optics and allowing for the effects of wind and weather are combined to put the sniper in position to take his shot. Each sniper trainee learns to fabricate his own 'ghillie suit' for camouflage and to work as part of a two-man sniper/observer team.

Since stalking skills are so important, great emphasis is placed on learning to blend into the terrain without being spotted by the instructors, even at close range. Throughout the various stages of training, the students are constantly evaluated with a minimum of seventy-five per cent required on all aspects of the course to pass. All of the other training is, of course, designed to put the sniper in position to fire his weapon; therefore, he is expected to be able to deliver his shot accurately when the target is presented. A total of one thousand five hundred rounds of ammunition is therefore expended by each trainee during training to develop the precision shooting ability expected of a trained sniper.

The final week of the course is a field training exercise culminating in a three and a half day 'mission' combining land navigation, infiltration, escape and evasion, and sniping. So rigorous is the course that only between a quarter and a third of those beginning it normally graduate. Those who do make the grade, however, are highly regarded and any company commander is glad to have AMTU trained paratroopers under his command.

Although the various types of training covered in this chapter represent the most common special skills encountered among 82nd Airborne troopers, a complete listing would have to be much longer. Many members of the division, for example, have attended jump master or parachute rigger training, enabling them to help the division perform its primary mission of jumping into battle via parachute. Other members of the division have attended specialized mountain warfare, SCUBA or desert warfare training. For a large portion of the division, this specialized training is designed to make each airborne infantryman more effective at helping the enemy die for his country, which is, after all, the real purpose of the entire US Army.

APPENDIX

Many other books exist which do an excellent job of discussing US military equipment and hardware; therefore, lengthy discussions have been avoided about most of the items of equipment used by US paratroopers during their existence. However, a few items of equipment are so fundamental to airborne warfare that a basic understanding of their characteristics should help in understanding the limitations and advantages of the parachute, glider or helicopter-borne trooper.

Parachutes

In any discussion of airborne troops, the parachute – their basic means of entrance onto the battlefield – must be considered an absolutely critical piece of equipment. When the US Parachute Test Platoon was formed, the T-4, a modified Army Air Corps parachute rigged for use with a static line, was adopted for the parachute infantry. An Irvin design, the T-4 was equipped with a 28ft canopy. While the T-4 was worn with a large square back pack, the reserve chute was worn on the front of the chest.

The T-7 chute replaced the T-4 in 1941 and incorporated many improvements. First, the T-7 was purpose-designed as a static line parachute. The T-7 was also both more reliable and more controlable. Additionally, it opened very quickly, allowing jumpers to exit planes at a very low altitude. However, the T-7 was difficult to get out of very quickly, since it used three snap hooks, thus increasing the likelihood of injuries on a windy drop zone. To help rectify this problem, post-war T-7s incorporated a box-type quick release.

In the late 1950s, the T-10 became the standard US parachute. Very reliable, the T-10 uses a 35ft (10.6m) canopy with an anti-inversion net skirt. Rather than a box quick release, the T-10 uses ejector snap quick releases. A 24ft (7.3m) chest-mounted reserve chute is worn with the T-10. The T-10B is still used as a primary parachute by the 82nd Airborne Division.

Also used by the 82nd is the MC1-1B Steerable Parachute, which allows very accurate insertion of troops since it is so controlable. Like the T-10, the MC1 uses a 35ft diameter canopy with the anti-inversion net skirt. To allow it to be steered, however, it incorporates a cut gore design with steering lines. The MC1 is also static line deployed.

Helicopters

Although the parachute remains an important method for troop insertions, especially where clandestine raiding or recon parties are concerned, the helicopter offers the airborne/airmobile force far more versatility.

Helicopters did see experimental usage in the US Army before the

Female parachute rigger checks a cargo parachute. (*US Army*)

Helicopters of the 82nd Airborne Division being loaded aboard a transport aircraft. (*US Army*)

Korean War and were used for medevac and other limited missions during that conflict. Widespread use of the helicopter as a troop carrier did not occur, however, until the 1960s after the Howtze Board made its recommendations about airmobility. The helicopter which became the workhorse for US airborne and airmobile infantry was the Bell UH-1 Huey. The earlier UH-1B could carry eight fully armed infantrymen, the UH-1D twelve and the UH-1H fourteen. In Vietnam and on through the 1970s and early 1980s, the Huey was the primary troop transport in service with the 82nd's Aviation Battalion.

Though the UH-1H remains in wide usage, its replacement—the Sikorsky UH-60A Black Hawk—has entered service with the 82nd Airborne, receiving its baptism of fire during the Grenada invasion. Almost fifty per cent faster than the UH-1, the UH-60 can carry eleven fully equipped paratroopers normally and up to fourteen in special circumstances. Both the UH-1 and the UH-60 have at times been rigged to allow paratroopers to jump with parachutes.

Though very important for granting airmobility, helicopters may be even more important to the 82nd Airborne as flying artillery. Though Hueys were altered in Vietnam to serve as gunships, it was the deadly AH-1 Huey Cobra which really proved the devastating firepower a helicopter could deliver. Armed with a combination of miniguns, 40mm grenade launchers, 2.75in rockets, TOW and other stores, the Cobra has increased the staying power of airborne troops immensely by offering on-call destructiveness hovering nearby. The current version of the Cobra, the AH-1S, has remained in service with the 82nd Airborne, though the new McDonnell Douglas (Hughes) AH-64 Apache, which incorporates highly sophisticated avionics and weapons, is now entering service with the division. Among the armament for the AH-64 is the Hughes 30mm M230A1 Chain Gun, which has a magazine capacity of 1,200 rounds and fires at the rate of 625rpm. The weapon wings carry four weapon pylons which can support a combination of Hellfire anti-tank missiles, 2.75in rockets or external fuel tanks for even greater range.

Although the parachute and the callused foot remain the primary means of insertion for the troopers of the 82nd Airborne Division, the very organization of the division as a light, highly mobile striking force makes the All Americans especially well-suited for helicopter deployment. As a result, only the 101st Airborne (Air Assault) places more stress on airmobility than the 82nd Airborne.

Aircraft

To be dropped by parachute, the paratrooper needs transport aircraft, and the troopers of the 82nd have been fortunate throughout their history to have had available some of the best troop transports in the world.

During World War Two the Douglas C-47 Skytrain (a military version of the DC-3) was by far the most widely used paratroop transport, carrying twenty fully equipped airborne troops into battle. Later in the war, the Curtiss C-46 Commando, which could carry thirty paratroopers, came into use but did not really supplant the C-47. One noteworthy advantage of the C-47 was that troopers could exit from both sides of the aircraft, thus speeding the drop and limiting scattering of the stick.

For a short time after the war, the Fairchild C-82 transport, which could carry 20,000lb (9,070kg) of equipment or forty-two paratroopers, came into use, but it was supplanted by the Fairchild C-119 transport in 1949. Able to carry forty-six paratroopers or 30,000lb (13,610kg) of equipment for a range of 1,770 miles (2,850km) the C-119 loaded through a tail gate, which allowed either troops or equipment to be dropped, thus adding versatility. Though the C-119 did not see combat usage with the 82nd, in Korea with the 187th Airborne Regimental Combat Team and in Indochina with French paratroopers, it was widely appreciated by airborne troops.

While the twin-boom C-119 was a definite improvement over previous transports as it allowed the troopers to jump rapidly from the rear ramp, or equipment to be pushed out over the DZ, it was the Lockheed C-130 Hercules which would become the primary transport of the 82nd Airborne for more than a quarter of a century. Able to carry sixty-four fully equipped paratroopers, who can quickly exit the rear of the aircraft in two columns, or 44,000lb (19,950kg) of equipment, the C-130 has a range of 4,460 nautical miles. With aerial refueling, the C-130 can drop troops of the 82nd Airborne anywhere in the world they might be needed. Not only that, but the C-130 can take off from unpaved runways as short as 2,000ft (610m) in length, making it useful for airlanding.

While the C-130 remains the principal paratroop transport at this time, even more paratroopers can be carried in the Lockheed C-141 Starlifter, which can carry 123 fully equipped paratroopers, who can jump from two doors at the aft end of the cabin. The C-141 is, however, most valuable for dropping heavy equipment, having set a world record by dropping over 70,000lb (31,750kg) on one flight.

Armored Vehicles

The M551 Sheridan Airborne Assault Vehicle came about as a result of the attempts in the 1950s to create a light tank with a gun capable of engaging enemy heavy tanks. The solution in the case of the M551 was the incorporation of an anti-tank guided missile which could be launched from the vehicle's smooth-bore gun, while HEAT (High Explosive Anti-Tank) caseless projectiles could also be fired.

The M551 was rushed into production by 1965, but it was not until 1968 that a really workable system for firing the caseless rounds was developed with the introduction of a closed-breech scavenger system to clear the breech of debris after firing. Problems with the ammunition, the gunsight and engine overheating continued to plague the M551, however. The recoil when firing the 152mm gun was also horrendous, lifting the vehicle a foot and a half off the ground and driving it a number of feet backward.

During service in Vietnam, the M551 had problems with the caseless ammo deteriorating badly in the humid conditions, engine trouble (especially overheating) and turret electrical power failures.

In 1971, the improved M551A1, incorporating a laser range finder, was introduced. The hull of the M551 is of aluminium, while the turret is of welded steel. The vehicle has a crew of four. It is 20ft 8in (6.30m) long, 9ft 3in (2.02m) wide and 9ft 8in (2.95m) high. Its weight is 35,000lb (15,875kg). Power comes from a six cylinder diesel engine. The 152mm gun can fire either the Shillelagh guided missile or various types of caseless ammunition. Additional armament consists of a co-axial 7.62mm machine gun and a .50 anti-aircraft machine gun. The M551 normally carries eight Shillelagh missiles and twenty rounds of HEAT or other types of 152mm caseless ammunition, 1,000 rounds of .50 ammunition and 3,000 rounds of 7.62 ammunition.

The 4/68th Armor of the 82nd has fifty-four M551s, which can be inserted via LAPES while the crew parachutes in. As this book is

Jeep-mounted TOW launcher and crew of the 82nd Airborne Division; this combination allows great mobility for the division's anti-tank capability. (*US Army*)

An M551 Airborne Armored Vehicle being loaded for a training drop. (*US Army*)

M551 Airborne Armored Fighting Vehicle extracted from a C-130 via LAPES technique. (*USAF*)

written, the 82nd Airborne remains the only Regular Army unit still using the M551.

Artillery

When the US airborne forces were first formed during World War Two, they were fortunate in having available for their gunners the 75mm Pack Howitzer, which had originally been developed to be transported by mules in rough terrain. The 75mm could be broken into nine components for parachuting and gave the airborne artillerymen a weapon capable of reaching out to 7,000yd. Although it could be parachuted, the 1,269lb (576kg) 75mm was usually delivered during World War Two by glider, which allowed the gun to be loaded already assembled and with its tow jeep and ammunition along with it. This excellent airborne gun remained in use with US airborne troops until the late 1950s.

The 75mm was replaced in the 82nd Airborne by the 105mm M102 Howitzer delivered via LAPES, heavy drop or helicopter. Weighing about 3,200lb (1,450kg) the M102 can range out past 12,500yd.

Beginning in World War Two, parachute troops found the lightness of the recoilless rifle attractive. It offered great weight savings for caliber, though the back blast generated by such weapons meant they needed a large clear area behind them, thus limiting their deployment somewhat.

Late in World War Two, the 75mm M20 Recoilless rifle, which fired a 14.5lb (6.6kg) HE shell to almost 7,000yd, yet itself weighed only 165.5lb (75kg) was issued in limited numbers to airborne troops.

The later 90mm and 106mm Recoilless rifles saw extensive use with the post-war airborne forces. At only 287lb (130kg) in weight, the 106mm M40A1 Recoilless rifle could fire HEAT or other rounds out to almost 7,000m. This weapon, though now replaced by TOW, in its time gave good anti-armor penetration—450mm at 1,000m with the HEAT round.

To combat tanks, the paratroopers' traditional nemesis, the World War Two All Americans had the glider-delivered 57mm anti-tank gun. Capable of penetrating 73mm of armor at 1,000yd the 2,810lb (1,275kg) 57mm had a range of over 10,000yd. Though incapable of stopping a German Panther or Tiger head on, it was certainly more potent than the bazooka.

During the 1950s and 1960s, the 106mm Recoilless rifle already mentioned gave paratroopers a compact yet effective tank buster. The ability to deal with tanks has, however, continued to receive high priority in the 82nd Airborne. The 66mm M72 LAW (Light anti-tank weapon), replaced the relatively ineffective bazooka as an individual anti-tank weapon. The 2.2lb (1kg) rocket of the LAW has an effective range of about 300m and can penetrate 300mm of armor.

Currently, however, the TOW and Dragon anti-tank missile systems are the major anti-tank weapons in the 82nd arsenal. The TOW launcher weighs only 172lb (78kg) and can be broken down and parachuted into battle with its operators. Its 42lb (19kg) wire-guided missile can range out to 3,750m to deliver its 5.3lb (2.4kg) shaped charge of HE with deadly effectiveness. The Dragon launches a lighter 13.5lb (6.1kg) missile which carries a 5.4lb (2.45kg) linear shaped charge out to about 1,000m.

AIRBORNE DIVISION

Mission

a. Movement by air and by airborne assault to seize and hold assigned objectives, to close with the enemy and destroy or capture him in an unsophisticated or semi-sophisticated environment until ground link-up can be accomplished or until reinforced by air or surface landing.

b. Movement by air and by airborne assault, when reinforced, to seize and hold assigned objectives in sophisticated operational environments.

c. Execution of small scale airborne commando type operations to perform selected missions.

d. Movement by air on short notice to any overseas land areas as a deterrent or resistant force in any threatened area.

Assignment

To theater or army group.

Capabilities

a. Execute airborne assault by means of parachute drop or air-landing.

b. Close with the enemy and destroy or capture him, utilizing fire, maneuver and close combat.

c. Conduct sustained combat for periods up to thirty days against an unsophisticated or semi-sophisticated enemy without major reinforcements.

d. Conduct all types of sustained ground operations when augmented by additional combat, combat support and administrative support units.

e. Act alone or as part of a larger force.

f. Conduct airmobile operations.

g. Individuals of this organization, except chaplain and medical personnel, can engage in effective coordinated defense of the unit's area of installation.

h. For mobility of the components of this division, see Section I, General, of each applicable TO&E.

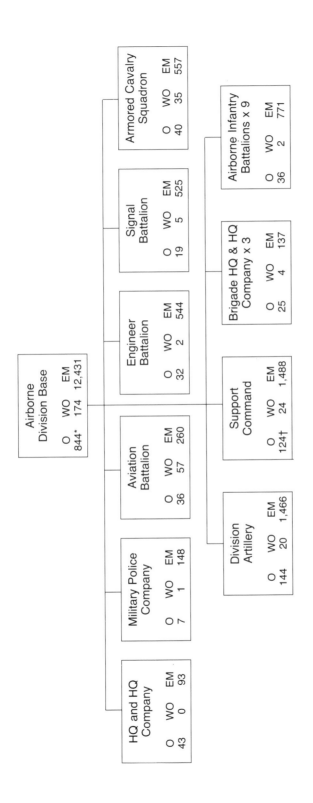

Airborne Division Base — O 844*, WO 174, EM 12,431

- **HQ and HQ Company** — O 43, WO 0, EM 93
- **Military Police Company** — O 7, WO 1, EM 148
- **Aviation Battalion** — O 36, WO 57, EM 260
- **Engineer Battalion** — O 32, WO 2, EM 544
- **Signal Battalion** — O 19, WO 5, EM 525
- **Armored Cavalry Squadron** — O 40, WO 35, EM 557
- **Division Artillery** — O 144, WO 20, EM 1,466
- **Support Command** — O 124†, WO 24, EM 1,488
- **Brigade HQ & HQ Company x 3** — O 25, WO 4, EM 137
- **Airborne Infantry Battalions x 9** — O 36, WO 2, EM 771

Notes

* Includes five (5) Officers Army Nurse Corps.
† The support commander's responsibilities for the Administration Company are limited to tactical, security and movement aspects.

Key

O: Officers   WO: Warrant Officers   EM: Enlisted Men

AIRBORNE DIVISION BASE
SUMMARY OF EQUIPMENT

Armament

	Division HQ and HQ Company	Aviation Battalion	Brigade HQ and HQ Company × 3	Signal Battalion	Military Police Company	Armored Cavalry Squadron	Engineer Battalion	Division Artillery	Support Command	Infantry Battalion × 9	Total Division
Machine Gun 7.62mm light flexible	—	—	2	2	8	42	17	69	29	24	389
Machine Gun cal .50 heavy flexible	—	—	—	—	—	11	—	—	8	7	82
Howitzer towed 105mm	—	—	—	—	—	—	—	54	—	—	54
Launcher grenade 40mm	—	—	9	15	13	59	71	60	2	85	1498
Mortar 81mm on mount	—	—	—	—	—	6	—	—	—	9	87
Pistol automatic cal .45	28	115	37	23	43	115	98	142	57	248	2849
Revolver Cal .38 4in 661	—	148	4	—	—	78	—	16	11	—	265
Rifle 106mm on mount	—	—	—	—	—	12	—	—	—	12	120
Rifle 5.56mm with bipod	114	205	121	525	111	439	479	1470	1567	561	10323
Rifle Recoilless 90mm	—	—	2	—	—	—	—	—	—	—	6
Armament Subsystem Helicopter 40mm Grenade Launcher	—	6	—	—	—	7	—	—	—	—	13
Armament Subsystem Helicopter 7.62mm Machine Gun Door Mounted	—	25	—	—	—	6	—	—	2	—	33
Armament Subsystem Helicopter 7.62mm Machine Gun 2.75in Rocket Launcher High Rate	—	6	—	—	—	7	—	—	—	—	13
Armament Subsystem Helicopter SS-11	—	—	—	—	—	4	—	—	—	—	4
Armament Subsystem Helicopter XM27	—	—	—	—	—	9	—	—	—	—	9
Flame Thrower Portable	—	—	1	—	—	—	—	—	—	—	3
Mortar 4.2in on mount	—	—	—	—	—	—	—	—	—	4	36

Vehicular

	Division HQ and HQ Company	Aviation Battalion	Brigade HQ and HQ Company × 3	Signal Battalion	Military Police Company	Armored Cavalry Squadron	Engineer Battalion	Division Artillery	Support Command	Infantry Battalion × 9	Total Division
Boat reconnaissance pneumatic 3-man	—	—	—	—	—	—	11	—	—	—	11
Crane shovel wheel mounted 7-T ½ cu yd gas driven 4×4 with boom crane 24ft block tackle 9-T	—	—	—	—	—	—	—	—	3	—	3
Grader road motorized diesel driven 10,000lb 12ft blade with leaning front wheels	—	—	—	—	—	—	4	—	—	—	4

AIRBORNE DIVISION BASE
SUMMARY OF EQUIPMENT

Vehicular

Item	Division HQ and HQ Company	Aviation Battalion	Brigade HQ and HQ Company × 3	Signal Battalion	Military Police Company	Armored Cavalry Squadron	Engineer Battalion	Division Artillery	Support Command	Infantry Battalion × 9	Total Division
Loader scoop type diesel driven 4 wheels 1½ cu yd	—	—	—	—	—	—	4	—	—	—	4
Tractor FT low speed diesel driven light air transmission	—	—	—	—	—	—	6	—	—	—	6
Transporter air mobile hydraulic lift for shelter 8×4 container	—	—	—	—	—	—	—	—	20	—	20
Trailer basic utility 2½-T w/e	2	7	—	—	—	—	—	—	—	—	9
Truck platform ½-T 4×4	—	—	—	3	—	1	—	24	3	41	439
S trailer van expandible 6-T 4 wheel w/e	—	—	—	—	—	—	—	—	4	—	4
S trailer stake 12-T 4 wheel w/e	—	—	—	—	—	—	—	—	3	—	3
Trailer ammunition 1½-2-T 2 wheel w/e	—	—	—	—	—	6	6	—	—	—	6
Trailer cargo ¼-T 2 wheel w/e	12	7	9	59	17	37	37	23	36	38	517
Trailer cargo ¾-T 2 wheel w/e	12	26	10	26	2	30	24	93	103	14	463
Trailer cargo 1½-T 2 wheel w/e	1	2	1	2	—	—	5	16	18	4	79
Trailer tank water 1½-2-T 2 wheel w/e	2	2	—	—	—	4	4	13	11	4	76
Truck ambulance ¼-T 4×4 w/e	1	1	—	—	—	6	6	1	4	6	104
Truck cargo ¾-T 4×4 w/e (192WWN)	13	29	10	60	2	36	52	161	110	14	719
Truck cargo 2½-T 6×6 w/e (70WWN-1 × LWB)	1	15	—	4	—	15	7	33	38	8	188
Truck dump 2½-T 6×6 w/e	—	—	—	—	—	—	27	—	—	—	27
Truck tank fuel service 2½-T 6×6 w/e	—	—	—	—	—	2	2	—	—	—	2
Truck lift fork diesel driven 4,000lb capacity w/e	—	—	—	—	—	—	—	—	7	—	7
Truck lift fork diesel driven 10,000lb capacity w/e	—	—	—	—	—	—	—	3	—	—	3
Truck tractor 5-T 6×6 w/e	—	—	—	—	—	—	—	—	7	—	7
Truck utility ¼-T 4×4 w/e	18	9	12	59	30	81	27	141	52	35	768
Truck wrecker crane 2½-T 6×6 WWN w/e	—	—	—	—	—	1	—	3	—	2	6
Truck wrecker light 2½-T 6×6 WWN w/e	—	—	—	—	—	—	1	—	—	—	2
Truck wrecker ¾-T 4×4 w/e	—	—	—	—	—	—	—	—	—	5	5

AIRBORNE DIVISION BASE
SUMMARY OF EQUIPMENT

Air Vehicles

	Division HQ and HQ Company	Aviation Battalion	Brigade HQ and HQ Company × 3	Signal Battalion	Military Police Company	Armored Cavalry Squadron	Engineer Battalion	Division Artillery	Support Command	Infantry Battalion × 9	Total Division
Helicopter observation OH-6A	—	4	1	—	—	9	—	9	9	—	34
Helicopter utility UH-1B	—	6	—	—	—	11	—	—	2	—	19
Helicopter utility UH-10	—	27	—	—	—	6	—	2	—	—	35

Command, Surveillance and Detection

	Division HQ and HQ Company	Aviation Battalion	Brigade HQ and HQ Company × 3	Signal Battalion	Military Police Company	Armored Cavalry Squadron	Engineer Battalion	Division Artillery	Support Command	Infantry Battalion × 9	Total Division
Detector kit cml agt line G4300	1	1	—	—	—	—	—	4	1	—	7
Detector kit cml agt line G4437	1	—	—	—	—	—	—	—	—	—	1
Detecting set mine portable metallic	—	—	—	2	—	—	32	—	—	3	61
Detector mine airmobile microwave	—	—	—	—	—	—	32	—	—	3	59
Detecting Set mine track mounted	—	—	—	—	—	—	1	—	—	—	1
Metascope assembly image infrared transistorized	—	—	3	—	—	14	—	—	—	27	266
Weapon sight infrared	—	—	—	—	—	16	—	—	—	10	106
Electric TT security equipment	—	—	—	—	37	—	—	2	—	—	39
Radar set AN/MPQ-4	—	—	—	—	—	—	—	3	—	—	3
Radar set AN/PPS-4	—	—	—	—	1	6	—	—	—	2	24
Radar set AN/TPS-25	—	—	—	1	—	—	—	—	—	—	1
Radiac set AN/PDR-27	2	3	2	2	3	5	15	13	16	4	99
Radiac set AN/PDR-60	1	—	—	—	—	—	—	—	—	—	1
Radiacmeter IM-93/UD	12	20	12	22	15	80	41	83	73	47	805
Radiacmeter IM-174/PD	3	9	7	6	4	46	23	26	15	26	387
Radio set AN/URC-10	—	—	—	—	—	—	—	—	2	—	2
Radio set AN/GRR-5	3	3	1	7	1	4	4	13	11	1	53
Radio set AN/GRC-106	4	4	4	4	—	4	4	13	13	1	53
Radio set AN/VRC-53	—	—	—	—	1	8	—	1	—	—	9
Radio set AN/GRC-125	2	—	—	—	—	25	—	—	62	25	314
Radio set AN/PRC-6	—	6	—	6	8	25	—	—	—	54	512

AIRBORNE DIVISION BASE
SUMMARY OF EQUIPMENT

Equipment	Division HQ and HQ Company	Aviation Battalion	Brigade HQ and HQ Company × 3	Signal Battalion	Military Police Company	Armored Cavalry Squadron	Engineer Battalion	Division Artillery	Support Command	Infantry Battalion × 9	Total Division
Radio set AN/PRC-25	3	11	11	—	—	34	40	16	1	55	612
Radio set AN/VRC-24	—	2	2	1	—	3	—	—	—	1	24
Radio set AN/VRC-46	9	4	4	14	21	21	15	70	21	20	385
Radio set AN/VRC-47	1	1	2	1	4	23	8	18	11	2	91
Radio set AN/VRC-49	—	2	1	9	1	3	1	4	1	1	32
Radio set con group AN/GRA-39	—	4	4	12	1	17	8	106	9	12	286
Radio set con group AN/GRA-74	—	3	2	40	—	3	3	3	1	1	55
RATT set AN/VSC-2	4	1	1	21	—	2	2	6	—	1	43
Speech security equipment TSEC/KY-8	—	—	3	3	—	2	2	9	—	—	30
Switchboard telephone manual SB-993/GT	—	4	1	—	—	—	12	18	6	5	81
Switchboard telephone manual SB-22/PT	4	—	4	8	4	4	2	19	6	6	100
Switchboard telephone terminal SB-86/P	—	5	2	6	—	—	—	2	—	—	14
Telephone set TA-1/PT	—	—	5	—	4	1	36	—	1	60	605
Telephone set TA-264/PT	—	—	—	—	—	—	—	3	—	—	3
Telephone set TA-312/PT	2	29	22	241	5	46	36	410	70	72	1553
TT set AN/TGC-14	—	1	1	2	1	1	2	2	—	—	9
Cipher machine TSEC/KL-7	—	1	—	9	1	1	—	2	—	1	30
TT set AN/TGC-15	1	2	1	—	—	—	2	1	—	—	8
Central office teletype writer AN/MGC-17	—	—	—	2	—	—	—	—	—	—	2
TT set AN/GCS-3	—	—	—	13	—	—	—	—	—	—	13
TT set AN/PGC-1	—	—	—	13	—	—	—	—	—	—	13
Control radio set AN/GSA-7	—	—	—	6	—	—	—	—	—	—	6
Control radio set C-2299/VRC	—	—	—	—	—	1	—	—	—	1	10

[**w/e:** with equipment]

BIBLIOGRAPHY

—*Airborne, Gung Ho Special* No 2 (1984)

—*American Armies and Battlefields in Europe: A History, Guide and Reference Book* (Washington DC: US Government Printing Office, 1938)

Antonia, Capt Keith. 'Pathfinder Training,' *Infantry* (Jan–Feb 1987, pp 34–5)

ARMY FORCES IN JOINT AIRBORNE OPERATIONS [FM57–10] (Washington DC: HQ, Dept of the Army, 1962)

Augsburger, Larry. *Vietnam II: 3rd Brigade. 82nd Airborne Division. January 1969 to December 1969*

Barry, Robert F. ed. *Power Pack* (Portsmouth, VA: Messenger Printing Co, 1965)

Blumenson, Martin. *Salerno to Cassino*. 'US Army in World War II' (Washington DC: US Army, 1969)

Bragg, R. J., and Turner, Roy. *Parachute Badges and Insignia of the World* (Poole, UK: Blandford Press, 1979)

Breuer, William B. *Drop Zone Sicily: Allied Airborne Strike, July 1943* (Navato, CA: Presidio, 1983)

Brucer, LTC Marshall. ed. *A History of Airborne Command and Airborne Center* (Sharpsburg, MD: Antietam National Museum, undated)

Carter, Ross. *Those Devils in Baggy Pants* (New York, NY: Appleton-Century-Crofts, Inc, 1951)

Chant, Christopher. *The Encyclopedia of Code Names of World War II* (London, UK: Routledge & Kegan Paul, 1986)

Coleman, John. 'One Shot, One Kill: Army Sniper School is Dead on Target,' *Soldier of Fortune* (Dec 1986, pp 44–51+)

Combat Record of the 504th Parachute Infantry Regiment (Nashville, TN: Battery Press, 1976)

Correll, Maj Jim. 'Golden Knights: Very Hot Stuff in a Competitive World,' *Gung Ho* (Jan 1984, pp 34–5)

Dank, Milton. *The Glider Gang: An Eyewitness History of World War II Glider Combat* (London, UK: Cassell, 1978)

Davis, Lt Forrest L. 'Countering Terrorism in the Trenches,' *Infantry* (Nov–Dec 1987, pp 31–5)

D-Day in Grenada: The 82nd Airborne Division in Action (Alexandria, VA: Photo Press, undated)

de Ste Croix, Philip. ed. *Airborne Operations: An Illustrated Encyclopedia of the Great Battles of Airborne Forces* (New York, NY: Salamander, 1979)

Devlin, Gerard. *Paratrooper: The Saga of US Army and Marine Parachute and Glider Troops During World War II* (New York, NY: St Martins, 1979)

—*Silent Wings: The Saga of US Army and Marine Combat Glider Pilots During World War II* (New York, NY: St Martins, 1985)

ESSENTIALS OF INFANTRY TRAINING (Harrisburg, PA: The Military Service Publishing Company, 1942)

Forty, George. *US Army Handbook, 1939–1945* (New York, NY: Charles Scribners Sons, 1980)

Galvin, John R. *Air Assault: The Development of Airmobile Warfare* (New York, NY: Hawthorn Books, Inc. 1969)

Garland, LTC Albert, and Smyth, Howard M. *Sicily and the Surrender of Italy,* 'US Army in World War II' (Washington DC: US Army, 1965)

Gavin, Maj Gen James M. *Airborne Warfare* (Washington, DC: Infantry Journal, 1947)

————'The Future of Armor,' *Infantry Journal* (Jan 1948, pp 7–11)

————*On To Berlin: Battles of An Airborne Commander* (New York, NY: The Viking Press, 1978)

Gregory, Barry, and Batchelor, John. *Airborne Warfare, 1918–1945* (New York, NY: Exeter Books, 1979)

Hamilton, Maj John. 'The Regimental System,' *Infantry* (Jan–Feb 1987, pp 20–24)

Harclerode, Peter. ed. *The Elite and Their Support,* Vol I (Hartley Wintney: Strategic Publishing Co Ltd, undated)

Harrison, Gordon A. *Cross-Channel Attack,* 'US Army in World War II' (Washington DC: US Army, 1951)

Hoyt, Edwin P. *Airborne: The History of American Parachute Forces* (New York, NY: Stein and Day, 1979)

Hudspeth, William. *Beret. Insignia of the US Army* (Hendersonville, TX: Richard W. Smith, 1987)

Huston, James A. 'The 82nd Airborne Division in Sicily,' *Infantry* (Jul–Aug 1985, pp 29–34)

————*Out of the Blue: US Army Airborne Operations in World War II* (West Lafayette, IN: Purdue, 1972)

INFANTRY REFERENCE DATA (Fort Benning, Ga: US Army Infantry School, June 1967)

THE JUMPMASTER [TC57–1] (Washington DC: HQ, Dept of the Army, Sept 1979)

Kahn, E., and McLemore, H. *Fighting Divisions: Histories of Each US Army Combat Division in World War II* (Washington DC: Zenger, 1980)

Laughlin, Cameron P. *US Airborne Forces of World War Two,* 'Uniforms Illustrated No 18' (Poole, UK: Arms & Armour Press, 1987)
Levesque, D. E. *Parachute Wing Ovals I.D. Guide* (Taunton, MA: David Levesque, 1980)

MacDonald, Charles B. *The Siegfried Line Campaign,* 'US Army in World War II' (Washington DC: Dept of the Army, 1963)
Mahon, John, and Danysh, Romana. *Infantry: Part I: Regular Army,* 'Army Lineage Series' (Washington DC: Office of the Chief of Military History, 1972)
Malloy, Capt Mike. 'Air Assault,' *Gung Ho* (Aug 1983, pp 36–45)
Marshall, S. L. A. *Night Drop: The American Airborne Invasion of Normandy* (Boston, MA: Little, Brown, 1962)
Mrazek, James E. *The Glider War* (London, UK: Robert Hale & Co, 1975)
Mrazek, Steven. *The 82nd Airborne Division: America's Guard of Honor* (Dallas, TX: Taylor Publishing, 1987)

Nichols, Nick. '82nd Airborne,' *International Combat Arms,* 'Guns and Ammo Action Series No 4'

Official History of 82nd Division American Expeditionary Forces, 1917–1919 (Indianapolis, IN: Bobbs-Merrill, 1919)
OPERATOR, ORGANIZATIONAL, AND DS MAINTENANCE MANUAL... PARACHUTE, PERSONNEL PACK (HALO) AND PARACHUTIST'S KIT, FREE-FALL (Washington DC: Department of the Army and the Air Force, Dec 1967)
Order of Battle of the United States Land Forces in the World War: American Expeditionary Forces (Washington DC: US Government Printing Office, 1931)
ORGANIZATIONAL AND DS MAINTENANCE MANUAL FOR GENERAL MAINTENANCE OF PARACHUTES (Washington DC: Dept of the Army, 30 Oct 1973)
Ospital, John. *We Wore Jump Boots and Baggy Pants* (Aptos, CA: Willow House, 1977)
PATHFINDER HANDBOOK (Fort Benning, GA: US Army Infantry School, Dec 1970)

Russell, Lee, and Mendez, M. Albert. *Grenada 1983,* 'Osprey Men-At-Arms' (London, UK: Osprey Publishing, 1985)
Ryan, Cornelius. *A Bridge Too Far* (London, UK: Hamish Hamilton, 1974)

Saga of the All American (Nashville, TN: Battery Press, reprint of 1946 ed)
Schnabel, James F. *Policy and Direction: The First Year,* 'US Army in the Korean War' (Washington DC: US Army, 1972)

Shults, Jim. 'Jungle Warfare School,' *Gung Ho* (Feb 1983, pp 40–5+)

Stanton, Shelby L. *Order of Battle US Army World War II* (Novata, CA: Presidio, 1984)

————*Vietnam Order of Battle* (Washington DC: US News Books, 1981)

Stubbs, Mary Lee, and Conner, Stanley Russell. *Armor–Cavalry: Part I: Regular Army and Army Reserve,* 'Army Lineage Series' (Washington DC: Office of the Chief of Military History, 1969)

TECHNICAL TRAINING OF PARACHUTISTS [TM57–220] (Washington DC: HQ, Dept of the Army, June 1986)

Thompson, Leroy. *Elite Unit Insignia of the Vietnam War* (London, UK: Arms & Armour Press, 1986)

————*Uniforms of the Elite Forces* (Poole, UK: Blandford Press, 1986)

————*United States Airborne Forces 1940–1986,* 'Blandford War Photo-Files' (Poole, UK: Blandford Press, 1986)

————*US Special Forces 1945 to the Present,* 'Uniforms Illustrated No 2' (London, UK: Arms & Armour Press, 1984)

————*US Special Forces of World War Two,* 'Uniforms Illustrated No 1' (London, UK: Arms & Armour Press, 1984)

Walsh, Frank. ed. *Dominican Crisis, 1965–1966* (Alexandria, VA: TBN, undated)

Weeks, Col John. *Airborne Equipment: A History of Its Development* (New York, NY: Hippocrene, 1976)

————*The Airborne Soldier* (Poole, UK: Blandford Press, 1982)

————*Assault From The Sky: A History of Airborne Warfare* (New York, NY: Putnam's 1978 and UK: David & Charles 1978)

Wildman, John B. *1982: Year of the 82nd* (Charlotte, NC: The Delmar Company, 1982)

Zaloga, Steven J. *US Light Tanks, 1944–84* (London, UK: Osprey Publishing, 1984)

Index

Page numbers in bold denote photographs